CADOGAN CHESS BOOKS

Soft Pawn

CADOGAN CHESS SERIES

Chief Adviser: Garry Kasparov
Editor: Andrew Kinsman
Russian Series Editor: Ken Neat

Other titles for the enthusiast include:

ELIE AGUR
Bobby Fischer: His Approach to Chess

LEV ALBURT
Test and Improve Your Chess

YURI AVERBAKH
Chess Endings: Essential Knowledge

JOSÉ CAPABLANCA
Chess Fundamentals

WILLIAM HARTSTON
How to Cheat at Chess

JULIAN HODGSON
Chess Travellers Quiz Book

DANIEL KING
How Good is Your Chess?

STEWART REUBEN
Chess Openings – Your Choice

VLADIMIR VUKOVIC
The Art of Attack in Chess

SIMON WEBB
Chess for Tigers

For a catalogue of CADOGAN CHESS books (which includes the Pergamon Chess
and Maxwell Macmillan Chess lists) please write to:
Cadogan Books plc, London House, Parkgate Road, London SW11 4NQ
Tel: (071) 738 1961   Fax: (071) 924 5491

Soft Pawn

William Hartston

Illustrations by Bill Tidy

CADOGAN CHESS
LONDON, NEW YORK

CADOGAN BOOKS DISTRIBUTION

UK/EUROPE/AUSTRALASIA/ASIA/AFRICA
Distribution: Grantham Book Services Ltd, Isaac Newton Way,
Alma Park Industrial Estate, Grantham, Lincs NG31 9SD.
Tel: (0476) 67421; Fax: (0476) 590223.

USA/CANADA/LATIN AMERICA/JAPAN
Distribution: Paramount Distribution Center, Front & Brown Streets,
Riverside, New Jersey 08075, USA.
Tel: (609) 461 6500; Fax: (609) 764 9122.

Published 1995 by Cadogan Books plc, London House, Parkgate Road,
London SW11 4NQ

© William Hartston 1980, 1995

Illustrations © Hutchinson & Co. (Publishers) Ltd 1980, 1995

First published 1980 by Hutchinson & Co. (Publishers) Ltd

British Library Cataloguing in Publication Data
A CIP catalogue record for this book is available from the British Library.

ISBN 1 85744 145 1

Cover design by Brian Robins (illustration by Bill Tidy)

Printed in Great Britain by BPC Wheatons Ltd, Exeter

For Elizabeth
and the bears

Contents

ACKNOWLEDGEMENTS

A project of this magnitude could hardly have been attempted without scorning the advice of too many people to mention here. Professor A. J. Ayer, Clint Eastwood, Anatoly Karpov and Tottenham Hotspur Football Club were but a few of those from whom words of guidance were not even sought. I should, however, like to offer thanks to my wife, who would have typed the manuscript had I not done so myself, and to Phillipa Walker who had the temerity to telephone Alan Coren on a matter concerning vultures and glass eyes.

Preface

'I wish to protest most strongly about everything.'
Letter from Henry Root to the *Evening Standard*

It has gone on far too long and the time has come to take a most serious stand on this issue. More and more hard chess books are becoming increasingly easy to obtain in our bookshops and on stalls at tournaments. Their explicit diagrams and lurid covers beckon the young player into their world of analysis and promised delights.

With the provocative appeal of a railway timetable these so-called theoretical manuals are influencing the youth of our country. And still the trains run late. I do not say that chess should only be played between consenting adults in private but let us bring back some dignity into chess literature.

To that end, I have produced this wholesome family chess book. Let no one claim that hard chess literature is a necessary part of our noble society before they have sampled *Soft Pawn*.

W.R.H.
Cambridge 1980

1. In the Beginning - A Fable

You have to kiss a lot of frogs before you find a prince.
Anonymous Wallscribe

Many years ago in a faraway Eastern land there ruled a powerful king, who was so rich and so strong that he was used to having everything he ever wanted. He was, in fact, the richest, strongest and most unutterably pompous and spoiled king there has ever been. But that was nothing compared to the arrogance and pomposity of his daughter, the beautiful princess, whose eyes shone with the brilliance of a Tal sacrifice, whose hair was as finely spun as a Petrosian strategy and whose skin was as smooth as a Karpov interview.

The princess was as beautiful as her father was rich. Some said she was more beautiful. Others stressed the inherent incomparability of beauty and riches, emphasizing the essential difference between value judgements of an aesthetic nature and precise measurements involving the weight of quantities of gold. The matter was never fully resolved despite the organization of philosophical symposia and debates on the subject; but I am sure you get the message: the princess was indeed *very beautiful*.

She had, however, one flaw in her character, which gave the king great cause for concern. Actually she had two flaws, but nobody was allowed to speak of the second following her conviction and suspended sentence for misappropriation of property, to wit one bowl of porridge, breaking and entering, malicious hooliganism and carnal knowledge of a bear. The cause of the king's grief was not this minor indiscretion in the past, but a far more worrying feature displayed by his daughter: the princess never laughed. The wisest and funniest men in the kingdom had tried to amuse the princess, but all had failed. Not so much as a chuckle could they raise from the sombre girl.

On her twenty-first birthday (it should really have been her sixteenth, but the princess was a late developer), the king announced a grand competition. Whoever could make the princess laugh would be rewarded with whatever he desired. The entry forms flowed in from far and wide. Contestants arrived by the coach load with their jokes, games and videotapes of old BBC comedy shows. But none could succeed in making the princess laugh, and they all forfeited their entry fees.

Then, late one dark night, there arrived at the palace a wizened old man, carrying a cardboard box and waving a crumpled late-entry form.

'I have invented,' he announced to the king, 'the most wondrously funny game, which is the only thing in the world that can amuse the princess.'

'What's it called?' asked the king.

'It is called chess,' replied the wizened old man.

'Doesn't sound very funny,' mused the king. 'Go on then, show us how it goes,' his majesty added, resignedly.

'Fetch a draughts board,' instructed the w.o.m. And the king summoned the Bearer of the Royal Draughts Board, who brought it forth from out of the royal games cupboard.

'Right,' said the w.o.m. rubbing his hands in glee as wizened old men are bound to do in stories such as this. 'Pay attention.' And he explained the rules in his wizened old voice, pointing to the pieces and squares with his wizened old fingers. But the king hardly listened. He had heard so many ideas to amuse his daughter, and this one looked a loser from the start. Plain daft, he thought it. Not funny at all.

Having at last come to the end of the rules, the old man paused and set the pieces on their starting squares.

'Now we must play,' he commanded.

The king was reluctant, for he had only really been listening as far as the pawn's move. He did not know how the other pieces moved at all. But the princess had heard all and was intrigued, in a morose way, by the complicated rules of this new game. She begged the king to take his seat at the board.

'Go on, dad,' she implored, 'it's good for a laugh.'

The king agreed, but on the one condition that he could have white. He thought for what seemed not very long at all and his hand alighted on the third pawn from the right. Cautiously he nudged it one square forward. The wizened old man moved his own king's pawn two squares up the board. Now the king felt that he was beginning to get the hang of it, so he moved the pawn second from the right boldly first one, then another square. The black queen shot immediately in reply to the end of her diagonal.

'Checkmate,' announced the w.o.m.

'Father,' exclaimed the princess, 'you are a twit. A ninny. A prize buffoon, a first-rate incompetent.' And she was smiling. Then the smile became a titter, the titter a laugh, and the laugh a full-throated guffaw. The outraged king hit her and she burst into tears.

But the king was an honourable monarch and told the wizened old man that the prize was his. Anything he desired, which it was in the king's power to bestow, he was free to request.

'Your Highness,' said the old man in a modest tone, 'I am but a simple peasant with few needs. I desire only the clothes in which I stand and some food to sustain me. I suggest therefore that you reward me at no great inconvenience to yourself by asking your agriculture minister to sign this document, thereby guaranteeing me one grain of rice for the first square on the chessboard, two for the second square, four for the third. . . .'

'Yeah, yeah,' said the king, 'and doubling all the time until you reach the sixty-fourth square. Well, hard luck; I've heard that one before. And I'm still paying off the guy who invented draughts.'

'Worth trying,' said the wizened old man. 'Okay, I'll settle for a beef curry, one poppadum and a weekend for two in Paris with the princess.'

'It's a deal,' said the king, and they shook hands. But from that day on nobody was ever allowed to smile while chess was being played. All who did so were officially considered mad and were shunned in polite society.

Time passed, and people forgot that chess was the funniest game ever invented. Only the princess remembered and she would always have a secret chuckle to herself when she saw men playing. The wizened old man, incidentally, had the misfortune to turn into a handsome frog when the princess kissed him. He whiled away the rest of his days hosting a television show. Some you win, some you lose.

2. An Astrological Guide

Nearly all professional astrologers are ignorant of their own subject, as of all others.
   Aleister Crowley, *Magick in Theory and Practice*

Before he gave up chess to become Britain's greatest authority on the Black Arts, Aleister Crowley was President of Cambridge University Chess Club, so he clearly knew a thing or two. Nonetheless, there is, in his writings, no direct reference to the profound influence of astrology on chess. This chapter remedies that important omission in our literature; I hope modern day astrologers and other ignoramuses will take due note of this important contribution to science.

We and the great cosmic chessboard are one. The planets are but pieces moving about on the surface of the cosmos, influencing our characters and destinies. The moment at which we are taken out of the box to join in the game of life is all-important. How the other pieces stand at that moment determines our fate. Now read on. . . .

Aries   (21 March – 19 April)

Aries is one of the fire signs, ruled by Mars, the planet of vigour, activity and energy-giving toffee-chocolate bars. As pointed out in the thirteenth century, people born under the sign of Aries tend to look like rams, with a hairy body, crooked frame, oblique face, heavy eyes, short ears and a long neck. Later, well-marked eyebrows were perceived as characteristic of this sign. This makes the Arien a formidable opponent; his hirsute face peering obliquely at the position, supported on an extended neck from a perversely bent frame is the ideal visage for intimidating the opposition.

The characteristic Aries personality is that of a fighter – aggressive, optimistic and belligerent. No surprise, therefore, that this should be one of the most propitious signs for chess-players, taking third place (behind Scorpio and Pisces, q.v. if interested) in the league table of grandmasters per sun sign. Smyslov is the only world champion produced by Aries; his eyebrows are sufficiently marked, but he would probably have held the title longer had his ears been shorter.

Maxim of the Month

> *Don't countergambit before it's hatched.*

Taurus   (20 April – 20 May)

Travel

Fate will soon take you on a journey to an unfamiliar place. You will there encounter a stranger, seated at a board of many squares, four and sixty in number, coloured alternately of light and darkish hue. Beware of this man; despite the apparent friendliness of his proffered handshake, his intentions toward your good self are nought but hostile. Follow the advice of the stars and treat him with circumspection, however, and the signs are auspicious that you will beat the hell out of him.

Money

Saturday and Sunday augur ill for dealings involving financial transactions. The prognosis is better for Monday, when the banks may well be open. Beware of tournaments to the East, where there is a curtain fashioned of iron, beyond which prizes are of a substance known as rouble which none can turn to gold.

Romance

'Twill be a goodly year for romance among chessplaying

Taureans. Much better than last year. Last year was really rotten, wasn't it? So was the year before that. You Taureans deserve a good year for romance after all you've been through. Everything comes to him who waits, though incipient senility may preclude his enjoying it to the full. Taureans should be most grateful to the author for predicting such a fine romantic prospect. I could have foretold even greater disaster than in the previous couple of years. But that would have been too depressing. And anyway, I only soothsay what I read in the cards. Sorry, that should read 'stars'. Palmistry or tea-leaves extra. Special cut-price offer on tea-bag readings this month only.

Motto of the Month

> *Ne'er cast a clout till you've got your knights out.*

Gemini (21 May – 21 June)

Inventiveness and intelligence are the characteristics of this sign, but you must control your jumpy tendencies to keep consistency in your results. Model yourself on the two Gemini world champions, Karpov and Petrosian, and you will not go far wrong.

Take special care in dealings involving rooks. Your lucky diagonal is g1-a7; your favourite colour is white; your propitious file is the QB-file. You need to work harder at the endgame, which you still do not play with sufficient accuracy. Your lucky opening is the Muzio Gambit, which is a really unfortunate piece of luck to have, because it has hardly occurred in tournaments since the turn of the century.

Providential Proverb

> *Black knight on high, eat shepherd's pie;*
> *Rooks in the morning, everyone yawning.*

(The origin and interpretation of this old farming saw are buried in obscurity. The second line is believed to refer to the undesirable practice of adjournment sessions being played too soon after breakfast.)

The Cancerian (sidelong stance)

Cancer   (22 June – 22 July)

This is one of the worst signs for a chessplayer to be saddled with at birth. Cancer has not produced a really great player since Morphy. This is hardly surprising when one takes into account the timidity and shyness characteristic of this sign. Also we must remember that crabs move sideways, whereas chesspieces are generally better advised to head forwards. Rooks born under the sign of Cancer are severely restricted by this handicap and can only make horizontal moves along the back ranks. Checking the birth dates of the rooks is an essential precaution before buying any chess set.

The best advice to give to chessplaying Cancer subjects is, in all honesty, to give up and look for some other direction in which to turn your sideways talents. If, however, you insist on persevering at chess, there are just two chances to overcome the problems of your birth sign. First, the study of opening theory can help compensate a little; Cancers have good memories combined with an understanding of current trends bestowed upon them by the moon, Cancer's ruler. The second, and I think, more ambitious remedy is to rotate one's chair through 90° before starting the game. The resulting sidelong view of the board can be enough to turn one's crab-bish qualities to advantage and ensure that the pieces move forwards. (The Swedish grandmaster, Ulf Andersson, used to adopt a related Cancerian panacea by sitting on his feet so that his body would not know which way was sideways. This was not totally successful, however, often leading to a complete lack of orientation manifesting itself in a horizontal shuffling style which only emphasized his Crustacean birth sign.)

Crab's Creed
> *A knight on the edge beats meat & 2 veg.*

(Whether Tarrasch knew this old proverb when making his own famous utterance about the value of knights at the edge of the board is a matter of some dispute. Since Tarrasch was a Pisces, it seems unlikely that he was familiar with the Crab's Creed, though some authorities differ on this point.)

Leo   (23 July – 22 August)

The sign of the Lion is without the slightest doubt the best sign of all. You are masterful, dignified, courageous, generous, honest, powerful and intelligent. You have wit, charm and personality, and your only possible weaknesses are a natural laziness which has resulted from your easy success, and a justified self-confidence which others (especially weedy Virgoans: q.v. if interested but it's hardly worth bothering) may misinterpret as arrogance. The author of this book, inci-dentally, is a Leo. His birthday is 12 August and as presents he likes to receive anything soft and cuddly including banknotes and fresh grouse.

Why then, you may be wondering, are not all the greatest

chessplayers huddled together under this exceptional sign? Despite our wonderful qualities, Leo only appears in joint sixth place in the league table of Zodiac signs for chessplayers. There are two simple reasons which fully explain this apparent paradox. Firstly, it is quite natural that many Leos should decide to be extraordinarily successful in some other field rather than waste their time beating up the representatives of inferior signs over the chessboard. Secondly, and more seriously for our prospects, the chessplaying Leo is phenomenally unlucky. His accident proneness is due to a wide selection of particularly unlucky squares over which he needs to keep watch during the game. Danger can strike without warning on any square of the. h-file as well as g4, f8, d4, b5 (or b2 from September to May) and various locations on the a-file depending on moon phase. A Leo entering a chess game needs the temerity of Biggles walking across a minefield. Really it is marvellous that we Leos can be as successful as we are, considering the ill fortune with which we are constantly plagued.

Leo's Law:

> *Many a swindle makes a nickel.*

Virgo   (23 August – 22 September)

If you thought Cancer was a bad sign for chessplayers, you should see the record of Virgoans. The last Virgo of World Championship class was Philidor around two centuries ago (and even that is a little unclear, what with calendar changes obscuring his true birth date). The best procedure to follow on discovering the sign of Virgo above your birth place is to unscrew it and make every attempt to dispose of it in part exchange for another birth sign. At current rates, anywhere in Eastern Europe, you should be able to trade in one Virgo for a slightly used Capricorn on payment of a pre-washed pair of jeans, a pack of gum, and a Clint Eastwood lapel badge. Any difficulties encountered in passing off the unwanted Virgo sign should be countered by mentioning some of the wonderful jobs which Virgoans do really well; like chartered accountancy or traffic wardenship. Better still, enlist the help of a friendly Leo to do the salesmanship for you. Leos are slick talkers who can sell anything to anybody. If you do not have a Leo friend, which is highly probable since Leos generally have nothing but contempt for Virgoans, then you could just find yourself stuck with your Virgohood. For such unfortunates all I can say is that the forthcoming year will be very average, reaching a peak of mediocrity towards the end of July, when you will draw several games from slightly advantageous positions. Do not push your luck, or you might even lose them.

Your favourite day is tomorrow; your lucky result is a win; your best opponent is another Virgo; your lucky football club is Nottingham Forest.

Helpful Homily

A passed pawn you push is worth two in the bush

Libra   (23 September – 23 October)

A difficult sign for chessplayers. The precision and harmony of Librans are good qualities, but their perfectionism and desire to weigh everything up before reaching decisions makes them particularly prone to time trouble.

The stars foretell a troubled year. Spasskiopeia in the house of Anatoly Centauri brings naught but havoc towards the end of January, but Olafsson's belt is on the ascendant and should keep matters in check. The Aurora of Korchnoi may be seen in the Western sky, but only from the front five rows which have been banned to spectators anyway. The emergence of the White Dwarf Kasparov in the heavenly canopy is predicted to lead to a total eclipse of the brightest star, Karpolis, within the next decade. The consequences for Librans could be nothing short of negligible.

So much for the long-range forecast. The chart for midnight tomorrow shows the Paroxysm of Petrosian in conjunction with the Appendectomy of Hort, bringing a deep depression spreading eastwards from Hendon. By breakfast time there will be much wailing and gnashing of teeth in NW6. Less

See a pawn and pick it up; drop it in his coffee cup

whaling, however, is expected off Reykjavik, following the activities of the International Whaling Commission and Greenpeace.

Your lucky piece is green. Your lucky motorway is the M4, which brings us home again to Wales where a welcome in the hillside can be confidently predicted after the pubs close.

Libran Lollipop

> *Happiness is a passed queen's pawn.*

Scorpio   (24 October – 21 November)

The characteristics of the Scorpio are invincible willpower, sharp minds and a passionate secretive intensity. Small wonder then that this sign produces more grandmasters than any of the others. The only trouble with this sign is the problem which arises if you play chess but have not attained the grandmaster title. Your date of birth cannot possibly be to blame, so you will have to look further afield for excuses. The following para-astrological explanations may be advanced in reply to any accusations that you are lacking in natural ability:

1. I was born on a cusp;
2. I was born on a bus. (No grandmaster has ever been born under the sign of London Transport – conceived in a taxi perhaps, but never born on a bus);
3. I was born in the Year of the Monkey (Chinese astrology is always worth a try if the conventional stuff fails to produce the goods);
4. The Tarot forbade it;
5. I have a toothache.

Scorpion Skulduggery

> *See a pawn and pick it up;*
> *Drop it in his coffee cup.*

(An ancient piece of advice, said to be extremely effective both in destroying an opponent's concentration and in ruining his coffee.)

Sagittarius (22 November – 21 December)

The useful features of this sign are ambition, cleverness and imagination, but inconsistency and lack of concentration can be a great drawback for the Sagittarian chessplayer. This sign has not been prolific in producing grandmasters, and can boast no world champion, but the great players born under Sagittarius, though few in number, include several candidates for the world title.

Sagittarians like horses, so if you are playing against one (a Sagittarian, not a horse) you should always take off his knights at the earliest opportunity. This will make him most disconsolate and he will play the worse for it.

If you are a Sagittarian and have had your knights taken, you may find that a member of the opposite sex can comfort you. Members of the opposite sex can be most comforting at moments of disconsolation. Apart from a cup of hot chocolate and a mild tantrum, there is little better when suffering from such vexation. Beware, however, of Sagittarian women, who tend to be loud and domineering. I can say this without prejudice, since some of my best friends are Sagittarian women.

Sagittarian Saying

Unzip a Benoni.

Capricorn   (22 December –19 January)

The sign of the goat. You are a solid, practical person with a long face and silly pointed beard. You are a founder member of the cud-chewing division of the even-toed ungulates. Not a great pedigree for a chessplayer, though Lasker and Keres were both goats.

The great advantage of being a Capricorn is the goat-like ability to leap over obstacles. While the Aries has to rely on butting away in blocked positions, the Capricorn can either butt or leap as he chooses. The laws of chess, however, were not drawn up with goats in mind, so much of the Capricorn's natural enthusiasm for bounding around has to be kept frustrated for the annoying reason that the rules insist on most pieces stupidly pushing their way along the board surface, bumping into things. Capricorns probably make far better draughts players than chess players, though figures are not available on this fascinating point.

In Mongolia, they cook goat by splitting open its back and placing hot coals in the cavity. Vodka in plenty is poured in and the resulting greasy mess of blood, alcohol and fat is then ladled out and drunk before it congeals. If you are a goat, you do well to avoid Mongolia at or near mealtimes.

Gastronomic Tip of the Month

What's sauce for the goose is a thick velouté enriched with egg-yolks, cream and garlic.

I hope this takes away the nasty taste left by the Mongolian goat.

Aquarius (20 January – 18 February)

Your lucky rank is the sixth rank; your lucky file is the b-file; your lucky diagonal is the long white one pointing upwards from b1. But beware! Your luck runs out at g6. Never push your luck as far as h7 or great ills will surely befall your position.

Aquarians wear odd clothes and are unusually prone to be struck by lightning. When playing chess out of doors during a thunderstorm, the Aquarian is therefore advised to keep his Wellingtons on, and on no account to seek shelter under a lightning conductor.

Aquarians are pleasant people with strong ankles who like fetching tea for their opponents. Do not accept their offers unless you are particularly fond of watery tea. Take special care at move twenty eight and on Thursdays. Always take your own roll of toilet paper if you play in the Soviet Union. Never trust a man with three Christian names. Always keep your socks on during a game.

Wise sayings

The pin is mightier than the fork; Procrastination is the mother of time-trouble.

Pisces (19 February – 20 March)

One of the most interesting zodiac signs for chessplayers. Pisceans are traditionally emotional, nervous and almost incapable of taking decisions. Yet Fischer (of course), Bronstein and Larsen, three of the most decisive and forthright players of modern times, were all born under the sign of the fishes swimming to and fro. This may seem odd, but the explanation lies in the very nature of chess itself. Pisceans are intuitive people, with a good understanding of the mysterious and intangible; just what you really need for chess, which is far too difficult a game for mere people anyway.

The Piscean chessplayer is well advised to rely totally on instinct. Do not try to calculate long variations, which you will probably get wrong in any case; study the board as if it were a restaurant menu and pick the move that tastes best. Play with your hands, not with your head. As David Bronstein once said, in reply to a question concerning how much of a particularly complicated variation he had analysed at the time of the game: 'You don't analyse during a game; you just play the moves.'

Tournament Tactic

> *Marry in Hastings, repent at leisure*

3. A Chess Bluffer's Manual I

I never read a book before reviewing it; it prejudices a man so.
   Reverend Sydney Smith

There are only two ways to secure a high reputation in the world of chess. The distinctly more onerous of these involves the consistent playing of good moves. As a medium for demonstrating one's mastery of the game, the board and pieces are, in fact, most unreliable. For that reason, the reader is strongly advised to take the alternative course and rely solely on the spoken and written word. With a little study he will find himself able to gain the esteem usually reserved for only the greatest of his brother practitioners. To impress others, the pen can be mightier than the pawn. This chapter begins the lessons.

Lecture One: The Great Masters

This is the first of three lectures which together comprise a complete course in chess bluffing. I have distilled all the information essential to give a picture of complete chess erudition. We begin with the biographies.

Of all the celebrated names in chess, six stand out way above the rest, to be revered with unstinting admiration. No word of criticism may on any account be levelled against any of the demi-gods to whom this chapter is devoted. On even less account should their names ever be uttered in the same breath as those of lesser mortals. We shall deal with them in chronological order.

PHILIDOR, André Danican (1726–95)

Adoration of this great man is currently unfashionable, thereby adding to his value as a conversation piece. By modern standards he was not a particularly good player, but others around at the same time were generally so abysmally poor at the game that Philidor looked superhuman. Actually his name was not Philidor at all. Louis XIII called him that when he was going through a funny phase of naming musicians after an oboist called Filidori. If you are bad at remembering names, it is a useful trick to call everybody Philidor, but you need to be a King to get away with it.

When not playing the oboe at Versailles or playing chess to supplement his musician's income, Philidor spent his spare time composing operas, one of which was even revived recently for performance in England. When talking about Philidor, his music may safely be praised since hardly anybody has ever heard any of it. If you have the misfortune to find yourself in the company of one who has encountered a Philidor motet or two, cast doubt on his credentials by suggesting that his Philidor was in fact the father of our Philidor. There were several members of the Danican-Philidor stable who composed around that time, so one can safely mention the bagatelles of C.P.E. Danican-Philidor, or the pin-ball machine of Wolfgang Amadeus Danican-Philidor.

'Pawns are the soul of chess' is Philidor's most-quoted remark. But here too lie the seeds of doubt since in old French the word 'pions' could mean either 'pawns' or 'peasants'. One could thus make a reasonable case for Philidor as an early French revolutionary, advocating power for the workers and peasant control of the means of chess production.

If cornered on Philidor's chess, mention his blindfold win against Captain Smith in which ten of Philidor's first sixteen moves were with pawns.

MORPHY, Paul (1837–84)

His middle name was Charles, which not many people realize. Morphy was famed for his combinational brilliance though it was really the soundness of his attacking play which was so unusual for its time. Morphy shot to the top of the chess tree in the United States then took a trip to Europe where he beat up all the world's best players with some ease.

All was going well until Morphy suffered a mortal blow to his pride when an American girl refused his proposal of marriage because he was only a chessplayer. Rather than do the sensible thing and jettison the young lady in favour of one with better values, he took the rejection to heart, gave up chess and tried to gain acceptance and fame in his profession as a lawyer. Great success in that sphere eluded him, he developed a paranoid attitude towards chess and died of apoplexy fifteen years after giving up the game for good.

Followers of the Freudian School of psychoanalysis cite

WHADDYA SAY, GENTS. WINNER PLAYS THE PHANTOM OF THE OPERA!

Morphy as a case-book example of the Oedipus complex in chessplayers. Practitioners of this vile game are trying to kill the father-figure (the king), which they unconsciously loathe and fear, with the aid of the powerful mother-figure (the queen) whose love they want for themselves alone. The chess game is the sublimation of the unconscious desire to commit patricide, latent in all men, so they say.

But they have it wrong, of course. The queen, as anyone can see from its strident mode of gallivanting about the board, is quite definitely male. The king, on the other hand, is too mincing in his movements to be a father-figure. At best a distant uncle or perhaps an effeminate cousin. The most famous Morphy game was played in a box at the Paris Opera. Morphy had the white pieces against Count Isouard and the Duke of Brunswick, consulting about their moves. The opera was *not* the *Marriage of Figaro*. When referring to this game, suggest a hint of doubt about the number of Morphy's opponents. It has never been definitively stated that these were really two different men rather than a single player who held both titles. Historians could easily have been misled by failing to consider the latter possibility.

LASKER, Emanuel (1868–1941)

The first point to note is the spelling of Lasker's first name. Once you have mastered that, you are well on the way towards becoming an authority on the man. His greatness as a player may be judged by the fact that he was the first to be accused of witchcraft at the chessboard. He was also accused of using psychological tricks such as deliberate bad play to unnerve the opponent. Just imagine how well you have to play for people to think that the bad moves must be deliberate.

Since Lasker, of course, witchcraft has become quite common in tournament play, though the recent FIDE ban on the slaughter of sacrificial beasts at the board has brought some decrease in activity.

The other important innovation for which we must thank Lasker is money. Before he applied his great brain to the topic, it had not occurred to chessmasters that they ought to use their talents for financial reward. Even for some time after Lasker it was considered rather bad form for a chessplayer not to die starving and penniless. Despite his good sense on this matter, Lasker ran into trouble with the hyper-inflation of the 1920s. He was already an ageing ex-world champion, but returned to chess to make some amazingly good results. His performance in finishing third at Moscow 1935 at the age of sixty-seven is perhaps the greatest-ever feat of chess longevity.

When not playing chess, Lasker studied philosophy and mathematics. Mention some of his contributions to the theory of Vector Spaces if you feel like a digression in the conversation. Remember to toast his birthday every Christmas Eve.

ALEKHINE, Alexander (1892–1946)

Alekhine was everything a chessplayer ought to be: an arrogant, selfish, alcoholic womanizer, with a talent for making enemies and a liking for cats. When sober he had a complete strategic mastery of the game and an unsurpassed ability to keep control of complex positions. This mastery became exaggerated when he published notes to his own games. He liked to include long variations, often discovered in analysis days after the game was played, claiming that he had seen them and calculated them correctly at the time. Sometimes too he would substitute a pretty finish which might have occurred for the more mundane ending which really happened.

Some tournaments he played with a higher than recommended level of alcohol in his blood. This led to reports of strange behaviour such as urinating in the corner of the stage during one event. After Dr Euwe had deprived Alekhine of the World Championship, the great man gave up drink, subsisting only on milk for two years until he had taken his title back.

Alekhine introduced hatred into the acceptable repertoire of match players. Against Capablanca in their 1927 match, there were periods when Alekhine refused to sit at the same board as his opponent. Karpov and Korchnoi adopted similar policies more than fifty years later, but nobody has ever really rivalled Alekhine for sheer personal venom.

To become a true Alekhine authority it is best to concentrate

on his losses. Firstly this is easier, since there are far fewer of them than his numerous wins, but also they are generally less well known. Some of his worst games, usually dismissed as aberrations of inebriation, nevertheless contain some remarkable original ideas. Had he but been sober enough to follow them up correctly, the whole of chess theory might have developed more quickly.

TAL, Mikhail (born 1936)

Tal was the youngest world champion ever and one of the very few real chess geniuses. He only held the title for a year, but the briefness of his tenure was due mainly to ill health. For this reason it is important to know his medical background correctly.

Firstly, and completely irrelevantly, Tal has only three fingers on his right hand. This congenital deformity might almost have been designed to lift chess pieces. Five fingers only get in each others' way. Tal's problems have always been caused by a troublesome kidney. Once this was removed his results over the chessboard began to improve again, but he had suffered a decade of rather inconsistent play.

Talking about Tal poses certain difficulties owing to the strong temptation to use the word genius. Tal himself always correctly points out that that particular term shoud be reserved for Bronstein. Had Bronstein not made the unfortunate mistake of failing to win the world championship, he would probably have taken Tal's place in this list and we would not have this trouble.

Never refer to Tal as a Russian. He is the Latvian World Champion. (Latvia is first right when you get to Estonia.)

FISCHER, Robert James (born 1943)

There is no doubt whatsoever that Bobby Fischer is the greatest of all. Anyone pretending to hold opposite views should be treated with extreme condescension. On no account should one indulge in argument with such illiterates for they will always be impervious to reason. When talking of Fischer, one should also steer clear of the delicate question of his sanity. Such problems as he may have are clearly subordinate to his enormous creative achievements, and should be correspondingly ignored. Any comments on his play should be limited to the words, 'Aah, Fischer', followed by a wistful, slightly demented look into the far distance.

Owing to his special position, Fischer's games should not be treated in the same manner as those of other players. As with the works of Mozart, the only human with whom Fischer may sensibly be compared, a catalogue has been prepared of the games of the great American. Just as Köchel did the job for Wolfgang Amadeus, Wade and O'Connell collected all Bobby's creative masterpieces. Thus one does not need to go to the length of describing a game as, for example, Fischer–Spassky, sixth match game, Reykjavik 1972. One simply says O'C 755 and everybody knows that you are referring to the game of that number in the Wade and O'Connell catalogue. A typical conversation between two Fischerophiles ought to run something along the following lines:

'Just came back from a play-through of O'C 444. The Ruy Lopez, do you know it?'

'Ah, yes. Typically early Fischer; you recognized, of course, the quotation of thematic material from O'C 72.'

'How true. And doesn't he give us a tantalizing foretaste of O'C 702, the first great Ruy Lopez from his late period?'

'Poor old Stein never stood a chance.'

'Aah, Fischer.'

'Aah, Fischer.'

And both end the conversation staring blissfully through each other in trances of Fischerian ecstasy.

4. The Case of the Mental Detective

The human brain is a device to keep the ears from grating on one another.
    Peter de Vries

'Ah, Watson! Good of you to come.' Sherlock Holmes opened the great oak door of his Baker Street chambers to admit his old friend. 'I've just received an invitation to present the prizes at the Slough Grandmaster Tournament. Knowing of your interest in chess I naturally decided to take the opportunity to invite you to accompany me and meet some of the players.'

'Jolly thoughtful of you, Holmes,' said Dr Watson eagerly. 'I'm not at all busy at the moment and would be delighted at the possibility to renew my acquaintance with the old game and its protagonists. When do we leave?'

'Straight away,' said Holmes decisively. 'Anticipating your enthusiasm, I took the liberty of booking seats on the 18.48 from Paddington. I can inform you of the tournament results on the journey and perhaps we might look over some of the better games from the bulletins.'

In the course of the short train ride, Watson learned more details behind Holmes's unusual alacrity in acquiescing to officiate at the prize-giving. The tournament had ended with a most remarkable result: in the first place was the American grandmaster Pescatory, who had won all eleven games to finish with a 100 per cent score. The other eleven grandmasters had all finished level on five points to share the remainder of the prize fund. Even for the great Pescatory this was an outstanding performance. Already, results such as these, combined with Pescatory's extravert, highly confident nature, had made him one of the most universally despised figures in the chess world. Holmes had, however, always maintained excellent relations with the great American and was delighted with the opportunity to present him with the large cheque and the famed 'Golden Rook of Slough' trophy.

During the journey Holmes had demonstrated to Watson the eleven crushing victories which had earned Pescatory his first place. Watson was not especially enamoured of the winner's own contemptuously dismissive notes to his opponents' moves. 'Refreshingly objective observations' was how Holmes had described them. Watson's opinion was that the man was a despicably arrogant example of a trans-atlantic culture, but this he left unspoken.

On arrival at Slough, the pair took a cab to their hotel, where the games of the tournament had also taken place and the players were still accommodated. As soon as they had reached their room. Holmes administered himself a quick shot of cocaine, then took out his violin and started playing some wild Hungarian music. Watson picked up the telephone, demanded room service and ordered some Italian food. Within minutes, the waiter had arrived bearing an almost unidentifiable pasta dish.

'Is that meant to be Spaghetti Bolognese?' queried Watson with a hint of incredulity.

'Brute Philistine,' replied Holmes, by now flying high as a kite. 'I thought that even you should be able to recognize the sound of a Szigeti Polonaise.' But before Watson could work his way back into the conversation, the telephone rang.

'Sherlock Holmes's suite,' announced Watson into the mouthpiece. A choked voice issued from the phone. 'For God's sake, come quick. I need help.'

'I think it's for you,' said Watson, handing the receiver to Holmes. The great detective carefully put down his violin and spoke loudly into the telephone.

'Sherlock Holmes, the great detective, at your service'.

'Thank God you're there. You're my only hope,' continued the voice. 'Come at once or it could be too . . . ' The voice stopped abruptly and the line went dead.

'That was Pescatory,' said Holmes.' I believe that he may be in some danger. We must hurry.' He swept out of the room with Watson managing to keep but a short distance behind. The waiter stood bemused in the doorway, still holding the spaghetti. After a brief pause he shrugged his shoulders and settled down to eat it.

The door to Pescatory's room was ajar when Holmes and Watson reached it. They rushed in, not pausing to knock, but were already too late. The body of the American grandmaster lay face down in the middle of the floor. From his back emerged the handles of eleven knives, each of distinct pattern from the rest, and all embedded to their hilts in the corpse of the unfortunate grandmaster.

'A dastardly crime,' said Holmes gravely, 'but we must not let our emotions interfere with our capacities for making logical deduction. Our task must now be to find the killer and bring him or her to justice.'

'Or them,' interpolated Watson.

'Don't be pedantic,' admonished Holmes.

'Well anyway,' continued Watson, 'this one doesn't look too difficult. Even I can make a pretty fair guess what happened here.' Even as he spoke the sound came drifting faintly from farther down the corridor of an eleven-voice male choir singing 'Ee-I-Addio, we won the cup'. Holmes, immersed deeply in his own thoughts, did not notice the noise.

'We are not in the business of making guesses, Watson,' he said critically. 'Criminal detection is a precise science. First we must find the murder weapon.' Watson blinked in disbelief at the body lying porcupine-like on the carpet.

'Those knives . . .'

'You don't eat spaghetti with a knife, Watson. If you must still think about food, may I recommend a visit to the kitchens for the purpose of acquiring a fork and spoon. As I was saying, there are no spent cartridge cases on the floor. I noticed that as soon as I entered the room. So he was not shot. No; by the angle at which the body lies we may safely deduce that he was bludgeoned to death by a blow or blows to the head with a blunt object.' His trained eyes scanned the room in a search for the likely weapon. Watson, whose legs were beginning to feel weak, sat on the edge of the bed dumbstruck, still staring at the pin-cushion of a body.

'I have it!' exclaimed Holmes suddenly. 'The typewriter. He was battered to death with the typewriter. Nothing else is possible. Find the owner of that typewriter and we have our murderer, Watson.'

'But my dear Holmes,' interpolated the doctor, unable any longer to hold his peace, 'that is Pescatory's own typewriter. He was, after all, a chess journalist as well as a player. And it's got his name on it in big capital letters on the top.' The great detective, however, was not listening. He was absorbed in a minute inspection of the supposed murder weapon.

'From the keys on this machine, I see under close inspection that some are worn considerably more than would be expected from the normal distribution of letter frequencies. We should normally expect the most used letter to be the lower-case letter e, which indeed it is also on this example, but here I fancy it is used still more than one would expect. And several other letters also admit to a similar description. Take down the following as I say them, Watson.'

Reluctantly the doctor extracted a pencil from his breast pocket and he wrote as the detective dictated: 'Capitals K,Q,R,N, and B and lower-case e,a,d,f,g,h,c and finally b.'

'Now consider,' went on Holmes with ever-increasing enthusiasm. 'What does that tell us of the owner of the typewriter and his occupation?'

'As I said,' replied Watson emphatically, 'he was a chess journalist.'

'A ludicrous guess, Watson, based upon not the slightest evidence. I am astonished that you can venture such an ill-thought opinion when it is perfectly obvious that the man we seek is a sailor!' Watson spluttered a few inconsequential monosyllables. 'Let me explain,' continued Holmes, 'though I should hardly have thought it necessary in view of the clarity of the evidence before us. Consider, good doctor, what are the letters used most frequently by the owner of a typewriter?'

'Well, in this case,' replied Watson, 'I should have thought . . .'

'You should indeed,' confirmed his mentor. 'The letters most frequently called into employment on any typewriter are those which are to be found in the very name of its owner. Those very letters which he utilizes perforce every time he fills in a form or writes a letter. In these capitals K,Q,R,N,B and lower-case e,a,d,f,g,h,c,b, we have, in enigmatic form admittedly, the very autograph of our killer.'

'The well-known sailor,' added Watson with a touch of cynicism.

'At last you have seen it. I congratulate you,' cheered Holmes grasping and shaking the hand of the bemused doctor. 'As you must have by now spotted, the five capitals are too many to be merely initials. Two or more of them must be in some way an appurtenance to the name, a title, degree or somesuch. And the only possible such suffix from the available letters is RN. Our man is a member of the Royal Navy, a sailor, Watson.'

'But that is not all the clues the typewriter can tell us', continued Holmes, warming to the task. 'Since there is no letter u, the Q must be a middle initial, and furthermore the proliferation of letters near the beginning of the alphabet, particularly f,g,h,e and a, tell us that he is an Irishman. Only a Gaelic name can have such a rare combination of letters. Possibly some such name as Keffeagh, which is, as you will know, my good doctor, an old Gaelic precursor of the present-day English names Keith and Kevin. Without doubt, he is an Irish sailor.'

Suddenly Holmes stopped and stared at the carpet where Watson's foot had been idly and dispiritedly swinging to and fro, creating an ever-deepening furrow in the pile between the body and the bed. 'How could I have missed that?' asked the great detective, rhetorically.

'Oh, sorry', apologized Watson. 'Didn't realize I was spoiling the carpet.'

'Only one instrument can be responsible for making such a single-track groove in Axminster pile,' carried on Holmes, oblivious to the doctor's interjection. 'Our man must have been riding a unicycle at the time of the crime! And to bring down a typewriter with sufficient force to kill Pescatory, while riding a unicycle, would demand that our killer be at least six feet eight inches tall.' Holmes paused, apparently unable for the moment to pursue his logic any further. 'What puzzles me,' Watson,' he continued slowly, 'are these remaining letters. We know his name is Keffeagh Q., something-beginning-with-B and the surname contains a further c,d and b, perhaps multiply, as well as possible further representatives from a,e,f,g, and h. Perhaps something like Keffeagh Q. Badbacache, but I would surely have remembered such a name were there one in the Royal Navy.'

Watson just stared at the eleven knives still embedded in the late grandmaster. He was wondering how to draw Holmes's attention to them before the great detective made a complete ass of himself. Any plans he may have had, however, were shattered by another sudden Holmesian outburst.

'I have it, Watson. How could I have been so blind. Keffeagh Q. Bacdabb!'

'Bacdabb?' echoed the doctor. 'What sort of a name is Bac-dabb meant to be? Not another of your Gaelic specialities. Or do we have here a trace of Pictish with perhaps a Finno–Ugric maternal grandmother? You'll never convince me that Bac-dabb . . .'

'No, Watson. Not Bacdabb. Macnabb! Our man is named Macnabb, but he has a cold, so it just sounds like Bacdabb.'

As the great detective uttered the final part of his explanation a great sneeze broke out from behind the curtain. The drapes spread apart, revealing a six foot nine inch man, dressed in full naval uniform, who pedalled slowly towards the detective on a unicycle.

'Keffeagh Q. Bacdabb ad your zervice, Bister Hobes. Gon-gradulations, me boyo, on a foin piece o' dedegdiv worg. I'll gome guiedly; id's a vair gob.'

5. A Glossary of Useful Terms

I cannot be didactic
or lucid, but I can
be quite obscure and practic-
ally marzipan.
     Mervyn Peake

Backward Pawn   A pawn which, through defect in education or inherent lack of ability, makes a stupid move, Intelligence tests do not confirm the popular belief that black pawns
are more dumb than white pawns. Persistent crass stupidity
can lose a pawn all his friends. He is then known as an isolated
pawn.

Bad Bishop   One who consorts with actresses or those of a
theatrical persuasion. In the early days of the Reformation, any
bishop seen participating in the Stonewall variation of the
Dutch defence on Black's QB1 was liable to immediate
excommunication. Only centuries later, after discovery of the
Finchley Central (q.v.), was this variation expunged from the
Vatican's list of forbidden openings.

Blockade   A paramilitary manoeuvre to prevent the opponent from obtaining supplies or refreshment between moves.
This is simplest accomplished by an allied detachment strategi-
cally placed to form a long instant queue at the tea counter as
soon as they see him coming.

Capablanca   It is not generally known that this Cuban
World Champion was born in England under the name of
Whitehead. After an unsuccessful attempt to interest Bertrand

Russell in joint authorship of a work entitled *Principia Scacchistica*, he emigrated to Havana and Latinized his name. There he wrote the book on his own and called it *Chess Fundamentals*. After defeating Lasker for the World title, he acknowledged the helpful advice given by his Irish neighbour Al O'Keane; 'You'll never get anywhere with a name like Whitehead.'

Counterpoint   A musical device to help chessplayers add up their wins. Originally invented by J. S. Bach as a personal favour to Philidor to enable the latter to total his points between writing operas. Philidor later earned enough to buy a pocket calculator, which accounts for the relative lack of contrapuntal writing in his later works. His gratitude, however, is clearly shown in the mating combination known as 'Philidor's Legacy', which he bequeathed to Bach in his will. Unfortunately Bach was already some forty years dead by the time the will was read. We can but speculate on what a fine chessplayer he might have become had he lived long enough to inherit.

Deciduous   A term of abuse originally applied only to pawn formations. If a pawn structure is riddled with so many weak and isolated pawns that something is bound to drop off pretty soon, then the whole structure is termed deciduous. Later the expression was loosely applied to any bad position. By an etymologically interesting back formation, the term 'evergreen' was applied to the game Anderssen–Dufresne 1852. The ninth game of the 1951 Botvinnik–Bronstein match is known as 'The Deciduous Game'.

Diagonalization   The process of winning a game by means of a mating combination along one of the long diagonals. A bishop in Finchley Central (q.v.) is an essential prerequisite to diagonalization. The originator of this term is reputed to be the English mathematician and grandmaster Dr J. Nunn: 'If he takes my pawn, I'll diagonalize him.' (BBC tape, 3.10.78; wiped later the same day.)

"YOU'LL NEVER TAKE ME ALIVE, COPPERS!"

MAN
FOUND
DIAGONALISED!
POLICE
SEEK
BISHOP!

Dragon Variation   The name of this Sicilian defence variation has often been mistakenly attributed to a fanciful resem-
blance between the black pawn formation and the profile of a
mythical beast. This is all too whimsical to be true. A far more
convincing derivation is from the tendency for theoretical
arguments and analyses of this wretched opening to drag on
and on and on.

The Benoni, however, is indeed so called because the black
pawns look like a bunch of bananas. A single Benoni pawn is
correctly termed a benonus.

Finchley Central   To develop a bishop on the long diagonal.
The long diagonal was first discovered, and named after, the
Irish musician and explorer Lonnie Donegal, on a visit to
North London while searching for a short route from a1 to h8.
The term Finchley Central was later taken to Europe where it

appeared in early manuscripts in the corrupt form 'Finchentro' and later 'Fianchetto'. Bishops developed on long diagonals are said to be 'in Finchley Central' or 'Finchley Centralled'. Bishops on slightly shorter diagonals are said to be in Muswell Hill, Hendon or Golders Green according to the desirability of the diagonal. That the influence and power of Finchley Centralled bishops was known even before the Russian Revolution, is clear from Karl Marx's expressed last wish to be buried 'in Finchley Central'. He spoke metaphorically, of course, but the pall-bearers took him at his word. Unfortunately they were short of the correct fare on the Northern line and found themselves having to alight at Highgate.

Grünfeld's Defence   Colourblindness. Grünfeld had terrible problems with his eyes and invented his eponymous defence by pure accident. Trying, one day, to play the King's Indian, he mistakenly pushed the black QP one square too far on his third move. He blamed this error on a combination of his own short-sightedness and the brown-and-yellow squared board on which the game was played. All the squares looked green to him, and he could not tell the difference between Q3 and Q4. Nevertheless, the game turned out very well, and Grünfeld realized that he had created a fine new opening. Since he had invented it by pure accident, he felt that the opening ought not to bear his name, so he coined the descriptive term 'Green square' (or, in German, *Grünfeld*) Defence. The similarity to his own name he staunchly maintained to be total coincidence. When accused of Narcissistic nomenclature, Grünfeld's Defence was always colourblindness.

Half-passed Pawn   Thirty minutes after Pawn o'clock.

J'adoube   An expression denoting unwillingness to move the piece touched. The derivation comes from an old English phrase, 'Shut up', formerly the conventional response to: 'You've touched that piece, you've got to move it.' Later the introductory sentence was omitted by the aggrieved player, and the piece toucher would automatically say 'Shut up' without the need for prompting. This was taken into middle High Flemish where it appeared as *Schodop* and later came into old Northern French as *J'odeupe* or *J'adoube*.

Nichya   Russian for draw. The word was an attempt by Stalin to pronounce the name of the German philosopher Friedrich Nietzsche, whose advocacy of conflict seemed very peaceful by the great Leader's own standards. Hence the name came to signify any conflict which ended amicably. Following his invention of *Übermensch*, incidentally, Nietzsche attempted to market a game called *Überschach* for *Übermenschen* to play in their spare *Zeit*. The game took place on a vast board with huge pieces which nobody could lift. Commercial success eluded him and Nietzsche sank into a deep depression during which he wrote '*Also Schach Zarathustra*'. He cheered up when Richard Strauss bought the musical rights, and *Übermensch* comics became popular.

Pasadoble   1. An *en passant* capture made by a doubled pawn; 2. Two connected passed pawns.

Petrodollar   Prize money earned by Petrosian, said to have a major influence on the Soviet Union's balance of payments.

Rook Ending   A cryptic crossword clue reference to the letters OOK. Thus 'Start of Botvinnik's rook ending volume (4)' clues the word 'book'. Beware, however, if the number of letters in the answer is '(7,3,9)', when it is far more likely to be 'Smyslov and Levenfish' who actually did write a book on rook endings. Orthodox rook ending players prefer unleavened fish.

Troubled Pawn   When three pawns of the same colour find themselves standing on the same file, the one with trouble is the original resident who started life alone in his block, only to be joined later in the game by two unwelcome lodgers. His living space must now be shared between the doubled pawn and the trebled pawn. Hence the name.

Viola da Gamba Any opening variation in which either player sacrifices a medium-sized stringed instrument.

Zugzwang An ugly German word which on no account should be pronounced or even attempted in correct Teutonic fashion. There are only two acceptable ways to say this word in English: 'wugzang' or 'Volkswagen'. The latter is recommended as a good descriptive term for a state best avoided and from which it is difficult to extricate oneself having made the mistake of getting into it in the first place. Far better than being in Volkswagen is to be in Bentley or Daimler. But remember that whereas in Volkswagen any move is liable to be fatal, moving when in Bentley or Daimler can carry prohibitive fuel costs.

6. Etiquette for Chessplayers

Curtsey while you're thinking what to say. It saves time.
Lewis Carroll, *Alice in Wonderland*

Sadly behind us are the days when admission to a chessboard was only to be gained by gentlemen and those of fine and cultured habits. Since the regrettable extension to the hoi polloi of rights of entry, standards of behaviour have not merely slipped, but plummeted to reprehensible depths. The time has come to reassert the equity by which those of natural grace and elegance may demand at the very least a modicum of decorum in dress and act of the Socially and Culturally Underprivileged Majority (hereinafter referred to as SCUM) who infest the tournament scene.

To that end, we have pleasure in providing a useful guide to right and proper manners for the chessplayer in the most commonly encountered circumstances. Those to whom gentle birth has given natural polish, may regard the remarks which follow as a refresher course. Others, less fortunate, to whom fate has provided lower natal credentials, should study these notes with diligence, that they too might some day aspire to standards of dignity to be expected of a gentleman and chessplayer.

Upon Introducing Oneself to One's Opponent

Good breeding demands at the very minimum a brief but cordial exchange of salutations before the commencement of a chess game. If at all possible, a mutual acquaintance of the contestants should be prevailed upon to make the necessary introduction. Chivalry demands that the lower-rated player be presented to the higher-rated. Never introduce an international master to a grandmaster without first asking the grandmaster's permission.

A fraught situation can arise if no intermediary may conveniently be procured to conduct the ceremony of introduction. Under such conditions, it is permissible to make one's own introductive promotion. Should the opponent be seated at the board, one attracts his attention by drawing back one's own chair with the left hand, making just the hint of a squeak on the floorboards, while extending the right arm in greeting. The handshake pressure should be firm but gentle. A slight bow is acceptable, but smartly clicking the heels is considered the epitome of uncouth Teutonic oafishness. In the event of this being the first encounter between the players concerned, he with the higher rating has the privilege of requesting that the other divulge his name, with the polite inquiry: 'Who are you, then?' A genuine interest in the identity of his inferior should be demonstrated by cupping a hand round the right ear as he replies and saying: 'What?' followed by impelling the scoresheet in his direction with instructions to inscribe his name in legible capitals.

On Moving The Pieces

Grasp the piece to be moved firmly between forefinger and thumb (or, in the case of the knight, between middle finger and thumb with the forefinger resting lightly between the ears*), lift the piece clearly above the level of the other men on the board (but never more than half an inch higher than the king), and move it directly and briskly to the intended destination. To push, flick or nudge a piece forward is considered most unseemly. When making a pawn move, the little finger should be extended.

To effect a capture, the enemy man should be removed from the board with the left hand (little finger extended, of course,

*The knight's, not yours.

should a pawn be captured), prior to occupying the vacated square with one's own piece in the right hand. One-handed captures, with whatever juggler's virtuosity they may be performed, are to be avoided as ostentatious and vulgar. The Chinese Ping-pong opening, involving the launch of the King's pawn some twenty feet into the air before stroking it down onto K4, may be tolerated as a harmless oriental eccentricity.

Writing the Moves

On transcribing a knight move to the score-sheet, one must take pains to ascertain whether the knight involved is an hereditary baronet. In such cases, the appellation 'Sir' must be inscribed before the move, and 'Bart' added after the square to which said piece has journeyed.

Winning

When the opponent has perpetrated a crass error, thereby rendering his game immediately beyond the slightest hope of redemption, one may look at him, but never stare, in amazement. Should he not resign immediately, only the ill-bred will be seen to yawn or consult their watches. One is permitted, however, to extend an invitation to others to share the mirth one harbours at the opponent's poor play and to express their intense amusement by gathering round the board and pointing in ridicule at the unfortunate wretch.

On conclusion of the game, the winner should compliment the loser on his high standard of play as exemplified by some, if not the majority, of his moves. The victor ought also to proffer helpful advice to aid the further study of his defeated adversary thereby leading to an eventual improvement in his game. Magnanimity in victory should always extend to drawing the attention of the vanquished to his every error, however trivial, that he might better extirpate them from his future excursions into the chess arena.

On Losing

Throwing oneself prostrate onto the floor and beating the ground with one's fists is a shabby demonstration of petulance in which no gentleman should indulge. A certain restrained amount of dignified rancour is, however, permissible and indeed expected under these strained circumstances. A good wallow in self-pity is the privilege of every loser. Refusing to shake hands with one's vanquisher is, on the other hand, clear evidence of a want of good breeding, notwithstanding the extreme fortune without which his victory could never have been registered. Resignation should be accompanied by a pertinent congratulatory message: 'I hope that makes you happy, you smug bastard; there's certainly not much else in your flaccid, philistine existence to be cheerful about.'

On retiring to your room to throw objects at the wall, always remember to beware of ricochets.

Upon Others Losing

One's friends and colleagues should be treated with the utmost sympathy after losses. Black morning coats, tall hats, black gloves and tie should be worn. If a message of condolence seems appropriate, verbosity should at all costs be avoided. A brief commiseration, such as 'Hard cheese, old fruit', will be fully adequate. This particular phrase is especially suitable owing to its easy translation into outlandish tongues for the benefit of foreign folk.

Consoling lady chessplayers after defeat is one of the peripheral occupational duties of the gentleman chessmaster. When pressed into giving succour and helping bolster the moral fortitude of such a distressed damsel, one must ensure always that the lady in question is allowed a few minutes to herself following the defeat. These important moments will give her the opportunity to meditate upon her misery, to reflect on the deeper and more meaningful aspects of existence, to experience the pure suffering caused by a great grief, and to throw an almighty tantrum with much kicking, stamping and screaming.

On the Offering of the Draw

To a grandmaster: a draw may only be offered by an untitled player to a grandmaster from a position of tangible superiority. The correct phrasing to adopt on such an occasion is: 'Your grandmastership, might I be so bold at this juncture of the contest to beg to suggest in all humility, the halving of the point?'

Should the grandmaster himself propose a draw, a summary refusal is the height of impropriety. Declining is permissible only with due deference to the grandmaster's superior status. Thus: 'Though fully content to earn half a point against such a powerful adversary, I would be willing to invest that and more in the continuation of this contest, that I might exploit to the full the opportunities to learn more of this wondrous game, such as are afforded to me by the privilege of sharing a board with your good and illustrious self.

To the Queen or Prince of the Blood Royal: should the vagaries of the pairing system during a weekend tournament place one against the Queen (or a Prince or Princess of the Blood Royal), the correct form of a draw offer is as follows: 'May it please your Majesty (Royal Highness); with the profoundest veneration (greatest respect), Your Majesty's (Royal Highness's) most faithful (humble) and dutiful (obedient) subject (servant) craves leave to petition for a draw..'

A royal offer of a draw must not be refused except in case of death. Such an offer should immediately be accepted in writing formally in the third person.

Upon Being Asked to Spy for the Russians

The Cambridge chessplayer, astute, educated, refined and drunk on the heady wine of Shakhmatny Bulletin and Soviet opening theory, may frequently be approached by seedy Eastern European types and asked to spy for the Russians. Under such circumstances, one should not let one's political views overcome proper notions of respectability. The offer should be politely declined in such a manner as not to have deleterious effects on one's future Soviet tournament invitations. 'Sir, I regret that my proclivities are exclusively heterosexual, thereby disqualifying me from the post you suggest on grounds of occupational unsuitability' is a convenient response to extricate oneself without any risk of causing offence.

This simple mode of disentanglement is less efficacious on being visited in one's room during a tournament by a scantily dressed, alluring female representative of a communist state, exuding unashamed sexuality, her luscious body straining temptingly against the confines of her remaining garments. Such a callipygean temptress can offer to the young and susceptible Cambridge chessmaster an opportunity to behave with indiscretion. Whatever the provocation during such social visits, however, the true gentleman will never overstep the bounds of decorum; socks are not removed before luncheon.

The true gentleman will never overstep the bounds of decorum.

Concerning Sacrifices

There is an art and propriety in the offering of sacrifices to the opponent which requires a natural delicacy of disposition to comprehend. Be it correct or totally unsound, the amount of material sacrificed must be neither gaudily too valuable, nor miserably insignificant. An ostentatious sacrifice of queen or two rooks, while doubtless affording a crude pleasure to those of low birth among the spectators, will mark one as a vulgar fellow to be shunned by the higher echelons of society.

Always accept the offer of a piece or pawn by the opponent. However humble the giver, your appreciation of his goodwill can only properly be signified by taking what he is willing to sacrifice. No matter how blatantly erroneous the offer, never demean the dignity of the poor chap by uttering a deprecatory expression such as, 'I fear I rob you'. The receipt of the gift should, however, be acknowledged by a brief note of gratitude.

On Nonentities

Having become a famous player, one will frequently be approached by nonentities who will attempt to engage one in conversation, saying: 'You don't remember me, but . . .' Their presumption should be rewarded by immediate interruption with: 'Yes I do; I beat you in a simultaneous display but five years past; a Nimzo–Indian Defence if my memory fails me not. You should have played the rook to d8. A most egregious error.' Then walk briskly away, leaving the bystanders lost in admiration.

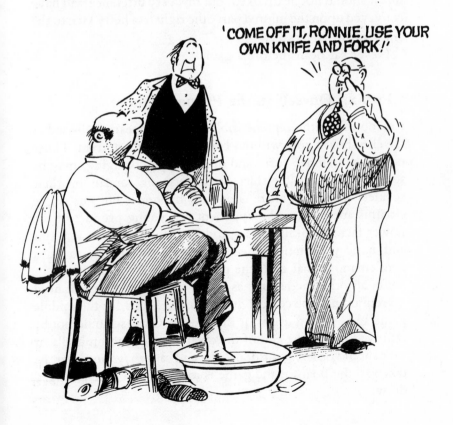

On Disgusting Habits

Certain players, not of good homes or family, indulge in certain vile and unmentionable forms of behaviour while seated at the board. These shabby and unseemly displays should not be tolerated. Should the perpetrator ignore your frowns and persist in his unspeakable ways, address him firmly thus: 'Sir, if you do not desist from your ungentlemanly ways, which I find injurious to both my concentration and my finer feelings, I shall have no alternative but to summon the tournament director and have you expelled.' This threat is the merest bluff, since the tournament director is in all probability at the very least a nose-picker, unsympathetic to the higher values of an aesthete. Should the opponent therefore respond unfavourably with: 'Sod you, mate', or similar phrase, the threat should not be invoked, but this very utterance will have conveyed upon the injured party the right to a hefty kick to the ankle of his adversary.

Never eat beans before a game.

Clothing Oneself in the Proper Manner

Far too often, the reprehensible habit of appearing ill-clad at the chessboard goes without being sufficiently decried. Those not to the manner born, and of slovenly upbringing, may be seen in jeans and tee-shirt, with decaying sandals on their sockless feet. Such attire is permissible under but one single circumstance: when the opponent is a young product of the Soviet factory, in his mass-produced, well-ironed natty suit and poncey imitation suede footgear, pretending to be a gentleman. In that case, the dirtier the tee-shirt the better.

On all other occasions, as every true gentleman will need no reminding, the correct dress is lounge suits for the middle game and evening dress for the ending. Gloves should not be removed before the end of the opening. Hat and umbrella or cane should be left at the door. Hat and cane may, however, be taken to the board if the game is to be a short, pre-arranged draw.

7. A Chess Bluffer's Manual II:

The Politico-Socio-Geographico-Cultural and Economic History of Chess

The thing is not beautiful, although it may still be waterproof.
Woody Allen

This second lecture in the trilogy of complete chess knowledge comprises a total guide to chess history from all conceivable points of interest. The separate phases of chess history may be clearly delineated and we deal with them in chronological order. Readers who prefer the traditional alphabetical order may rearrange the following material without any loss in clarity.

1. The Geographical Age   AD 550–1560

The earliest form of chess was a game called chaturanga played in north-west India. Persian and Sanskrit ballads of the mid-seventh century refer to this game so historians assume that it was invented about a hundred years earlier. What with the time it takes to sign up the strolling minstrel, wring a contract out of the publishers and correct the proofs, even in those days a century could pass before you had a book in the shops.

Chess was a slower game at that time, played exclusively by the aristocracy. The pieces on each side were a king, a counsellor, two elephants, two horses, two chariots and eight footsoldiers, with occasional guest appearances by dogs and camels. Since the queen or counsellor could only move one square diagonally and the bishop's move was also restricted, nothing much happened in the game. The problem of this era was how to transport such a ponderously lethargic game to Europe. But for two fortunate accidents, this geographical impasse might never have been surmounted.

The first accident happened during a Crusade. Richard the Lionheart was feeling bored on one of the rest days, so Saladin invited him over for a drink. During his visit the good King learnt the game of chess and brought it back to England. That incident is not fully authenticated but sounds convincing enough to be taken as true. Meanwhile, the other accident was that the Moors decided to go to Spain for their holidays, presumably because Morocco was fully booked. They took their chess sets with them and evidently left some behind. Thus, one way or the other, chess came to Europe.

2.   The Cultural Era   1561–1726

As soon as the game reached Italy, the Renaissance trendies decided to soup it up a little. The queen and bishops were given huge increases in power, pawns were allowed to move two squares on their first go, and castling was thrown in. The volatile Italians savoured the newly created violence of the game.

Despite this obvious pandering to popular taste, the upper classes maintained their exclusive rights to the game. To Philip II of Spain we owe the introduction of true culture into the development of chess. He was a keen player and, when asked what he wanted for Christmas 1561, he demanded a chess book. His favourite priest, Ruy Lopez, was consequently dispatched to Italy to buy one. While he was there, Ruy Lopez took time off to beat the leading Italian players and came home with a book by Damiano called *Questo libro e da imparare giocare a scachi et de li partiti*. This had been published in 1512 and had probably been remaindered by the time Ruy Lopez bought it. Anyway, the Spanish priest did not like the book at all, so on his flight home wrote his own work, entitled *Libro de la invencion liberal y arte del juego del Axedrez*. This came out just in time to put in Philip II's stocking.

They really knew how to name books in those days. Why is it that when there were only two or three chess books in the whole world they had titles a yard long, while now, with thousands on the market, they are all called *Chess* or *An Introduction to Chess* or some equally undistinguished title?

Back in sixteenth-century Italy, however, they were seething with rage because good old Ruy Lopez had beaten their best players and rewritten their book. After a dozen years training they sent a two-man hit squad consisting of Leonardo da Cutri and Paolo Boi to do for old Lopez. They duly arrived in Madrid and both beat the Spaniard in matches to retrieve their national honour.

3.   The Sociological Revolution   1726–1850

Chess was now becoming too important to be left to the aristocrats. The eighteenth century began to see the balance of power shifting towards artists and scientists. France had a surfeit of artists at the time, so several of them decided to dominate world chess. The great Philidor, who was the best player in the world from the day of his birth in 1726 until he died sixty-nine years later, was followed by Deschapelles and La Bourdonnais. Between them they reigned supreme for a century.

But already the chess epidemic was uncontrollable. Having infected the artists and scientists, nothing could stop its spread to the middle classes. And England, who had invented the middle classes, had a natural advantage over the more primitive nations. In 1843 Howard Staunton won a long match against Saint-Amant to bring the unofficial world championship across the channel. It may even be that this single occurrence was the reason for Saint-Amant's canonization; history is obscure on that issue.

4.   The Political Era   1851–1971

By now chess had been played for around 1300 years, but nobody had yet thought of holding a tournament. Staunton himself remedied this omission by arranging for all the world's best players to compete at London in 1851. All of Staunton's plans for the event went well, except for the fact that he only finished fourth. The winner was Adolf Anderssen, a man of somewhat Germanic persuasion. The modern era of chess as an international sport was truly under way, with all powerful nations of the world anxious to prove they were the best.

Naturally the Americans were quick to muscle in on the scene. They sent Paul Morphy across to win matches against all the greatest European players. Staunton, by a combination of quick footwork and good sense, avoided meeting the American, thereby keeping his own reputation reasonably intact. Morphy returned to America and never played again. This left the Europeans rather confused and suffering from a justifiable feeling of inadequacy.

The death of Morphy finally gave Europe back its sense of self-respect, which they cashed in by arranging an official world championship match between Steinitz and Zukertort. The latter is, I believe, some sort of sweet confectionery, so it should be no surprise to hear that the ravenous Steinitz won with consummate ease. That was in 1886 and the title was to stay in central Europe for many years in the hands of Steinitz and Lasker.

The next important event in chess history was the Soviet Revolution. Lenin was looking for a suitable way to honour his pledge of culture for the masses. It had to be cheap and had to be something he could understand. Not having had Marx's advantage of the British Museum library ticket, Lenin found his choices limited. In a moment of inspiration the Great Leader decided to give his people chess. They deserved it, and he played it quite well. Thus began mass chess education in the USSR.

Meanwhile, back in the West, chess theory was developing into a polemical debate. The squabbles which were taking place gave the Russians time to catch up. Dr Tarrasch was the man to blame. He was a humourless character with pince-nez, whose main intention was to take all the pleasure out of playing chess by reducing the game to a set of dogmatic principles. He confused the issue by playing much better than he wrote, but this seemed to fool his opponents and only made them angrier. He had been arguing with anyone who came his way, but his most concerted opposition came from the Hypermodern school, the Pre-Raphaelites of chess.

Reti, Breyer and Nimzowitsch* were the leaders of the hate-Tarrasch club. Breyer had all the good ideas, but died far too young. Reti was the most complete player, but Nimzo had the charisma and eccentricity to be Tarrasch's greatest opponent in debate. Among other odd pieces of behaviour, Nimzowitsch is reputed to have performed headstands on the stage of tournaments and would also wrap his leg tightly round the chair as an aid to concentration. Nobody knows whether it is true that he once broke his leg by standing up too abruptly when in such a pose. Such ideas were in any case far too hypermodern for old Tarrasch whose hairstyle was too immaculately greasy to permit headstands.

Back in Moscow, Stalin had assumed Lenin's mantle of the Great Theorist. His ideas for world domination were more practical and his great buddy Krylenko set to the task of a five-year plan for chess. By the time Stalin had him shot, Krylenko had really done quite well and the young Russians were well on the way to capturing the world championship. Just to make sure, Stalin annexed Estonia so that he could claim Keres as a Soviet player. But he need not have worried; Botvinnik won the title for Russia in 1948.

The next quarter of a century was dull. The Soviet Union went into the business of stock-piling ex-World Champions with Botvinnik losing to various people then regaining the title. By 1970 the USSR had one reigning champion and four ex-champions. But the political era was coming to an end.

5.   The Economic Revolution   1972–

Until 1972 it was considered poor form for a chessmaster to make any money from the game. If he died other than in

*Nimzowitsch himself was unsure how to spell this difficult name, but Keene has sorted out the problem for him.

penury he was hardly playing the game at all. Bobby Fischer changed all that. With the impertinence of Paul Morphy he not only beat all the best players in Europe, but he demanded and received goodly sums of money for doing so. Almost overnight an enormous change had come over the world of chess. Other players quickly followed his example and asked to be paid too. Of course, they did not, in general, receive so much at first, but the chess grandmaster suddenly became a piece of hot property desired by all men of wealth. By 1978, the prize and bribe fund for the World championship had increased tenfold even over 1972.

And so, as the twentieth century draws to a close chess has finally caught up with the modern era. Even the Russians are beginning to want more than roubles for playing. Perhaps we can all now afford to slow down a little.

8. Chess Club Drifter

If there's one thing above all a vulture can't stand, it's a glass eye.
Frank McKinney Hubbard

He never said where he came from, and few even dared ask. The tall man rode into Dodge City with only the clothes on his back and a chess set in his hand. All eyes were on the stranger as he strode into the saloon. Conversation came to a sudden stop and an ominous tension seized the smoky air as he pushed a dollar bill towards the barman.

'Gimme a drink,' said the stranger. 'Tea, no milk, one sugar.' The barman stood motionless, his hands pushing down on the bar, his eyes fixed menacingly on the face of the newcomer. After a few seconds which felt like minutes, the stranger spoke again. 'Please', he added defiantly. The barman's knees shook; he poured the drink, steaming from its pot, and pushed it towards the stranger. He pointed at the chess set.

'We don't hold with no chess playin' in this bar.' The stranger ignored him and threw the tea down his parched throat. His journey had been long and the warm drink was a welcome refreshment.

'Where's the chess club?' he asked, banging the cup back in place on its elegant Minton saucer.

'Are you lookin' for a game?' asked the barman. 'We don't want no trouble here. We're decent peace lovin' folk here in Dodge.'

'I asked where's the chess club?' repeated the stranger threateningly, fingering the sliding lid of his chess set.

'I'll take you there.' A voice from a corner table broke the silence. The old man who had spoken the words rose slowly and ponderously from his stool and began to make his way towards the stranger. 'Pleased to meetya, stranger.' He extended his hand in greeting. 'These young 'uns don't know no more how to treat a real chessplayer.'

The stranger's grey eyes narrowed to slits. His fingers grew more taut round the box of chessmen as he ignored the offered handshake.

'Used to push a pretty fair pawn m'self when I was shorter in the tooth,' went on the old man, unperturbed, 'but the old eyes ain't what they wuz. Where did you say you wuz from?'

'I didn't,' replied the stranger. 'Let's go.' And he led the way out of the saloon.

'You sure are mighty eager for a chess game,' continued the old man, urging his limbs to keep up with his new companion's brisk pace. 'Used to be eager m'self. Eager young Jess, they used to call me. Now they just call me old Jess, now that I'm not so eager and me legs don't seem up to it no longer. What did ya say ya name wuz?'

'Didn't say', replied the stranger. 'They call me Grandmaster.'

Old Jess and the man they called Grandmaster strode on together in silence. Old Jess led the way to the chess club with unwavering steps. He had made the journey many times before, long ago. They came over the ridge at sundown.

'Well, we gone as far as I can accompany ya,' said Jess, with a touch of sadness in his voice. 'The chess club's that shack down yonder.' His hand gestured towards an isolated cabin at the end of a long track. 'I'd come all the way with ya, but an old man like me ain't welcome down there no more. I don't stand no chance with them young 'uns. Not since the arthritics got at my moving finger. Used to be the fastest mover in Dodge before . . . '

His voice tailed off as he realized that he was talking to the dust and the flies. The man they called Grandmaster was already standing tall at the entrance to the chess club. With one quick movement he kicked open the door. Inside the room pieces froze in mid-move as all heads turned towards the doorway. They gazed in surprise at this fearless figure silhouetted there, a bishop in each hand, ready for action. The tense silence was punctuated by a dark unshaven man, with a star proudly pinned to his chest.

'If you're lookin' for a game, stranger, you've gotta pay the membership fee,' he said, with thinly disguised avarice.

The man they called Grandmaster looked at the badge. He made out the words 'Club Secretary' etched on its tin face.

'Don't hold with no membership fees.' He pointed his bishops menacingly. 'But I gotta little idea that might interest ya. Waddya say to a fair game, just me against you? If I win, you enrol me in the club. If I lose, you can have your membership fee.'

'Okay, stranger,' said the man they called The Club Secretary, as the other club members gave way to nervous talk and giggles. 'Just the two of us and no funny business. And I've got White.' He emptied a box of pieces onto a spare board. All others present shrank to the walls of the clubroom, knowing that wood was about to fly and afraid that they might get hurt. They knew that the secretary was the best player in Dodge City. He was never beaten, except in occasional away matches or when he wasn't feeling none too good or sometimes when the lighting was bad or the pieces too small. All eyes were on the chessboard as the game began.

Almost before the stranger had seated himself on his chair, a white pawn shot out and lodged itself in the wooden square known in Dodge as e4. The stranger did not even blink. More pawns were spat forward in rapid succession, then pieces followed. And suddenly it was all over. The Secretary lay slumped across the board, defeated.

A lone figure detached himself from the crowd to come forward and congratulate the stranger. His badge bore the legend 'Deputy Secretary'.

'Welcome to Dodge City Chess Club. We'll need your name for the records.'

'Just put down "Grandmaster",' said the stranger, putting the pieces slowly back in their box. 'That's what folks call me.' A hushed silence reigned throughout the room.

'Well, Mister Grandmaster,' continued the Deputy Secretary, 'now you're a member, I'd like to invite you to play for us next Saturday in the away match against Deadwood Gulch.'

You could hear the hiss of indrawn breath as the other club members winced in anticipation. No one had ever returned alive from an away match at Deadwood Gulch. They had No-socks McGuirk on top board, the man they called 'The fastest pawn in the West'.

'Sure, I'll play,' said the Grandmaster, 'for my usual fee.'

'And what might that be?' inquired the Deputy Secretary, suspiciously.

'A bottle of whisky, a woman, and a Clint Eastwood lapel badge. Double if I win.'

'Will the same woman twice do, or does it have to be two different women?' asked the deputy, thinking fast. It was his quick mind at times such as this which had got him the job. He had studied law.

'I'm not fussy,' said the Grandmaster.

'Okay, it's a deal,' agreed the Deputy, and he prepared a contract.

News of the Secretary's downfall spread like wildfire through the town. Wherever the grandmaster went they treated him with fear and respect. He was given the best room in the saloon, courtesy of the man they called the Manager. He took everything he wanted: whisky, women, morning papers, all charged to his room number. Some called him profligate. Others did not know what it meant. But none dared complain. In any case, they knew that after Saturday he would be gone.

They rode together into Deadwood. The Dodge City team come for the big match. The streets were deserted as they got out of the coach. It was clear they had been expected. All the local inhabitants were either at the chess club or cowering behind locked doors. The grandmaster led his team into the premises of the Deadwood Gulch Chess Club. Six boards lay sprawled across the middle of the room, each one set with its own chessmen. At the very far end sat No-socks McGuirk, glowering over the pieces. Slowly and cautiously the Grandmaster advanced, his shadow sliding across the board. He

drew back the seat opposite McGuirk. Never taking his eyes off his opponent, the Grandmaster sank into the chair.

'Ain't seen you around before,' said McGuirk.

'Ain't been here before,' replied the Grandmaster, uninformatively.

'Say, No-socks!' rang out a voice from the crowd, 'Who's the fancy dude with the Clint Eastwood lapel badge? Are you sure he's eligible for a Cowboys' Club Championship match?'

'That's true, mister,' said a small figure hiding behind a badge bearing the emblem 'Controller'. 'You've gotta play two or more games in serious competition for Dodge City in the Deadwood and District League before youse qualified for their Cowboys' Club Championship team. What's yer name? I'll go check the records.'

'Ain't got no name. They call me Grandmaster,' said the man they called Grandmaster.

'Youse gotta have a name. There ain't nothing in the rules 'bout players with no names,' protested the Controller.

'If I ain't got no name and there ain't nothin' in the rules then I cain't be ineligible,' said the Grandmaster in what was to be easily his longest sentence in the whole story. 'Let's get on with it.'

'Well I'll be horn-swoggled if that don't fail to make no sense,' said the Controller nodding his head. Then, totally bemused by his own negative-ridden construction, and unsure anyway what was meant by horn-swoggled, he decided to let them get on with it. 'Okay, No-socks; draw for colour.'

At the word 'draw', No-socks shot forward his right arm in a smooth almost reflex action, landing on the Controller's left wrist. He slowly prized open the fingers and a black pawn crashed to the floor. A faint smile crossed the lips of the Grandmaster. With the black pieces No-socks was as good as dead.

The match was a foregone conclusion. McGuirk thought long and fought hard, trying all he knew, but the Grandmaster was too quick for him. As No-socks became progressively more desperate, his lined and dusty face grew more streaked with rivulets of sweat. The bandana he used to mop his brow grew damper and dirtier. When his flag finally fell, No-socks McGuirk had in any case, run out of ammunition. The final score-line read 'Deadwood Gulch 5 Dodge City 1'. It was the best ever result for Dodge against their bitter rivals.

The Grandmaster collected his fee from the citizens of Dodge, and at dawn, began his long ride out of town. The rest of the city lay silent and mostly sleeping. The cable from the US Chess Federation waited unopened on the desk of the President of the Dodge City Chess Club.

'FOLLOWING PROTEST DEADWOOD CHESS CLUB REGRET INFORM YOU DODGE CONVICTED PLAYING INELIGIBLE MAN STOP DISCIPLINARY COMMITTEE HEREBY IMPOSE LIFETIME BAN ALL ACTIVITIES DODGE CITY CHESS CLUB STOP EQUIPMENT AND PREMISES CONFISCATED ALSO TWO POINT PENALTY DEADWOOD WIN FIVE TO MINUS ONE NO APPEAL STOP REGARDS USCF.'

It was the worst ever result for Dodge against their bitter rivals. No chess was ever played in the City again.

By the time the President opened the cable the Grandmaster was already passing the city limits. Old Jess was leaning on the memorial stone at the tomb of the unknown chessplayer which marked the boundary.

'Say, stranger, I been doin' some thinkin' an' I reckon we met someplace before, when I wuz a young 'un, and me knees wuz still bendin'.'

The man they called the Grandmaster rode past in silence and vanished into the mist. His voice filtered back to old Jess, still waiting and scratching his head: 'Mebbe we did, old man. Anything's possible.'

9. Victor the Second - Part One

A Tragedy

Dramatis Personae

VICTOR – a challenger
FIRST SECOND
SECOND SECOND ⎱ his attendants
THIRD SECOND
A CRONE
A GURU

Scene: Somewhere in the Philippines

Act One – Scene 1: *A room in the challenger's camp. Victor sits alone at the chessboard.*

VICTOR   My preparations are at last complete
this long-awaited battle to begin.
My plot to seize proud Anatoly's crown
is hatched. The prize is well within my reach.
My fingers itch to squeeze that scrawny neck
and from his greasy hair remove the jewels.
He calls himself a king although the throne
whereon he perches is itself maintained
by evil forces from an Eastern land
where once I dwelt but never shall return.
But wait, there's yet a little work to do.
I'll summon forth my valiant band of aides.
Come in, my seconds, we must analyse
the Nimzo-Indian and QGD.

   [*Enter three seconds*]

FIRST SECOND   And not just those sweet Victor, we must plan
foul strategems to disconcert the foe.

SECOND SECOND   I have some ready ruses to disturb
the equanimity of all who dare
combine their strengths our forces to oppose.

THIRD SECOND   Delve first, my liege into my bag of tricks
as ne'er in a menagerie were seen.
I speak of yoghurt and reflecting specs
and evil eyes and electronic beams.
Against such weapons no one can resist.

VICTOR   That sounds fair sport. If mischief be the game
I'll act upon vile Hecate's advice.
Come forth old crone

   [*Enter a crone*]

and tell me what the days
ahead hold for my prospects.

CRONE   Three months long
the battle will be fought and many wounds
sustained in the fight. But mark these words:
Look not upon the yoghurt when 'tis blue!
   [*Exit Crone*]

THIRD SECOND   What mean these words? I fear they bode no
good.

SECOND SECOND   Methinks the crone's completely out to
lunch.

FIRST SECOND   But soft! 'Tis possible the room is bugged
and Russian buggers★ hear our every word.

VICTOR   Then we perchance may play a merry jape;
with information false we'll ply their ears.

★In the First Folio this appears as 'rushing Bulgars', considered by some
scholars to be a reference to itinerant Bulgarian gentlemen visiting the Russian
camp.

Let's talk of king's pawn openings and such
defences which I have no mind to play.
And if our foes o'erhear thereby ensure
by their own bugs the buggers buggered be.

Scene 2:   *The same – two weeks later*

VICTOR   Six draws and now a seventh seems at hand.
  I thought this game was won and yet I erred
  when pressed for time and now the villain can
  escape. Where lies the cause of my poor play?

FIRST SECOND   Remember'st thou the words of Hecate?
  Methinks the answer's in his dairy foods.

SECOND SECOND   Nay that is not to blame. The reason lies
  in something parapsychological.
  Hast thou not seen that wicked staring face
  which sits each day upon the seventh row?

THIRD SECOND   We must protest upon't, and have him
  . thrown
  back to the chamber's rear where he belongs.
  I'll pen a missive to the arbiter
  Meanwhile put on these glasses which reflect;
  they'll turn his evil magic on himself.

FIRST SECOND   But don't forget the yoghurt in your note;
  for if complaint is menu for the day,
  be sure we do complaint both well and long.

VICTOR [*aside*]   These seconds do protest too much,
  methinks.
  See this position wherein I've adjourned.
  There's tricks yet to be found. Come analyse!

FIRST SECOND   That's best!

SECOND SECOND   Nay this! .

THIRD SECOND   No, something else instead.

VICTOR   Work well, dear friends. I'm shagged and off to bed.

Scene 3:   *Victor's bedroom, seven weeks later. Victor sits alone.*

VICTOR   My efforts have not captured much success.
Five battles have I lost, and won but two.
One more defeat will surely be my last.
Is my ambition to be thwarted thus
without a fight? That master of man's fate
appears to have it in for me betimes.
Those sixty-four vile squares have oft conspired
to dash my hopes and yet one chance remains.
If I can but four victories secure
before I lose again then all is well.
But how to tame that unresponsive wood
whereof the men who dwell upon my board
are fashioned? How to make them do my will?
Those kings, queens, rooks, knights, bishops, e'en the
        pawns
will ne'er do as they're bid. Those bishops foul!
Aye, 'tis the bishops do upset me most.
They practise their ecclesiastic walk
upon those vain diagonals of life.
There on c1 one smugly sits as if
to tell me I know not where he should move
and will not, should I wrack my very brain
another million years. Which square is best?
d2? e3? f4? g5? h6?
Or with a craven fianchetto end it.
b2 or not b2, that is the question.

   [*Enter a Guru*]

GURU   Say, man, what's all this uptight misery?
You know what's wrong? Your aura's all screwed up.
Like, transcendental meditation, man
is what you need to cool the current scene.

VICTOR   What says this apparition? His strange tongue
lies outside my experience, and yet

I feel there might be aught in what he says.
Speak on, good friend, I'll follow your advice.

GURU   Good thinking, man, together we can beat
this parapsychic mumbo-jumbo crap.
I'll teach you lots of mantras to recite,
and how to win by standing on your head.

VICTOR   Upon my head? Can this indeed be true?
I'll try it! After all, I lag five-two.

[*Exeunt, performing head stands*]

Act Two – Scene 1:   *A room in the challenger's camp, two weeks*
later. All enter.

VICTOR   Five two, five three, five four and now five five.
Like Banquo's ghost I've come back from the grave.

FIRST SECOND   We've got him now, just two more games
methinks;
one black, one white and then the trophy's ours.

SECOND SECOND   For once we're all agreed, the match seems
won;
and Anatoly's crown ripe to be plucked.

THIRD SECOND   Go out and draw today with pieces black.
The thirty-third game will foretell his doom.

VICTOR   This day my Pirc Defence will make him work
For half-a-point, and then on Friday morn★
with these same white men which today he holds
I'll break down his defences. Then the prize
for which we've laboured o'er these past long months
will be at last ensconced in my own hands.
Farewell, dear friends, I'm off to play the Pirc.

GURU   Keep cool, man, don't forget the headstand bit.

★Friday afternoon actually, but the demands of scansion transcend temporal
accuracy.

CRONE   When the battle's lost and won.
When the yoghurt's overdone,
Tooth of gerbil, eye of cat,
leg of Yorkshire's opening bat,
makes a magic foul and hairy,
warning that thou must be wary,
for the teabags do foretell
death for one we all know well.

[*Exeunt*]

Scene 2:   *But five hours later.*

FIRST SECOND   Oh dear

SECOND SECOND   Oh dear

THIRD SECOND   Oh dear

CRONE   I told you so!
You heeded not the warning in the tea.
And now you've paid the price and lost the match.

VICTOR   The match and all for which we fought so hard
are lost indeed. My destiny was not
so easily o'ercome. It seems I'm doomed
to rise not to the first place but must stay
at second. Yet I live to fight again.
So, gloating crone, your prophecy was false;
I am not dead. Yet may it still come true.
That death of which you spoke could be thine own.
    [*Takes dagger and stabs crone*]

CRONE   Oh perfidy, oh treachery, oh hell!

VICTOR   With that I'm freed from her pernicious spell.
Come goodly Seconds, I've still faith in you,
There'll be a better ending to Part Two.

[*Exeunt*]

10. The Chess Capability Inventory

You've got to get up early if you want to get out of bed.
  Groucho Marx.

The pages which follow contain some questions which our long and laborious studies and research have identified as able to detect differences between chessplayers and the general population. By combining items measuring intelligence with those giving indications of personality factors and attitudes, this short inventory has been found to detect latent chess disposition. Since chess is itself a part of our western culture, some of the items may be found to have a cultural bias. This should be borne in mind when filling in the answers. The pass mark is eight correct responses.

1. Which of the following letters is the odd one out?
   A E I K O U

2. Sometimes I think the whole world is ganging up against me.
   (a) true   (b) false

3. Complete the following sentence:
   Yesterday I won, today I win, tomorrow I.................

4. Which of the following numbers is the odd one out?
   450   451   453   456   459   462

5. Though my friends consider me conceited I am in fact much cleverer than I think.
   (a) true   (b) false   (c) I have no friends

6. Black to move in this position; what did he play?

7. A snail pushes a rook up a chessboard. It takes twenty minutes to progress two squares forward; then it sleeps for ten minutes during which time rook and snail slide back one square. Maintaining this schedule, how long does the snail take to move the rook from the first to the eighth rank?

8. Why is this position illegal?

9. Complete the following well-known saying:
The best form of defence is..................

10. Which is the odd one out?
French Defence, English Opening, Dutch Defence, Danish Gambit, Brussels Sprouts, Slav Defence.

11. Whose sixth victory on what occasion in 1978 ensured that he would retain his title?

12. I think this is a silly test and I'm going to stop after this question
(a) true   (b) false

Answers Score one for each correct response unless otherwise specified.

1. The correct answer is U. All the others are penultimate letters of the names of post-war World chess champions.

2. True. They *are* ganging up against you.

3. Celebrate. Deduct one point for 'shall win' which shows unwarranted presumption and a level of overconfidence bound to end in disaster.

4. 462 is the right answer; the others are all Köchel numbers of Mozart Piano Concerti. The cultured chessplayer ought to know that sort of thing.

5. (a) scores one point. If you answered (c) award yourself half a point if it makes you feel any better.

6. The position is from the game Popiel – Marco, Monte Carlo, 1902. Black should have played B – N8 (no points) winning at once. He actually resigned (one point) thinking his bishop was lost.

7. The snail never makes it to the eighth rank, it loses on time on the sixth rank.

8. It is parked on a double yellow line.

9. The Sicilian. Half a point for the Nimzo-Indian which is quite all right, but not so interesting.

10. Slav Defence. The others are all named after members of the European Economic Community.

11. Bjorn Borg in the final set at Wimbledon.

12. True.

11. A Chess Bluffer's Manual III

How to Succeed at Chess Without Actually Playing

How can someone who calls himself a logical positivist be a Tottenham Hotspur supporter?
    Letter to A. J. Ayer in the *Guardian*

We all know how difficult it is to impress people by playing chess. They always tend to judge by our results rather than appreciating the quality of our moves. This makes matters difficult since, owing to the natural perversity of the game, the result is not within the control of its practitioners. Chess is, in fact, largely a matter of luck and there is no way the congenitally unfortunate can gain success within its domain. This is simply demonstrated: in most positions nobody has the ability to calculate fully the consequences of any single move; we are therefore all stumbling around blindly hoping something will turn up. Thus good fortune is an essential ingredient of successful chess.

   The clarity and logic of this point are unfortunately lost on most people. Too easily they have been waylaid by the centuries of propaganda that chess is a game of skill. They are misled by the linguistic trick of referring to 'good' and 'bad' chessplayers instead of using the more appropriate designations, 'lucky' and 'unlucky'. Hence one must, as far as possible, avoid playing chess if the desire is to impress. It is too chancy. Fortunately, however, talking a good game is just as effective, if not more so, than playing one. The art is easily acquired with but a modicum of study.

The Opening

In the last hundred years a vast library of accumulated literature on chess openings has developed which the zealots study and revere. One is generally expected to be conversant with the latest opinions of the theoreticians if any attention is to be given to one's pronouncements. Keeping up with this great move factory is, however, a full-time job. Fashions change with every tournament and what one day was considered a main-line variation will the next be relegated to a footnote. This is all very confusing since no firm conclusions are ever reached about whether particular openings are good or bad. They just meander in and out of fashion at the whim of the trendsetters.

The only acceptable policy when talking about openings is one of non-committal omniscience. The conversation should proceed along the following lines:

'What do you think of Karpov's opening?'

'Really interesting. I'm so glad he played that. I was looking at it only last week; it's theoretically crucial, you know.'

'What do you think he'll play now?'

'I can't quite remember what I decided was the best move. I have all the analysis written down at home. There were so many complicated possibilities.'

'He's taken the pawn; is that an innovation?'

'I think not. I seem to remember Bronstein playing something like that in the 1950s.'

Almost anything may safely be attributed to Bronstein. He has gone through a long chess career with the rather depressing habit of thinking of most ideas about twenty years before they occurred to anyone else. If you fancy a change from invoking Bronstein, an equally apposite attribution would be to 'an old suggestion of Bondarevsky'. Alternatively one may quote obscure games from recent events. The Greek master Z. Grophulous may always be credited without fear of contradiction.

Writing about openings is a far more complicated matter. In general adding to the opening literature mountain is not to be recommended except as a possible cure for penury. For some reason books on opening theory do sell well. People seem to believe that they help.

The Middlegame

This is a portion of the game between the opening, where everybody is expected by familiarity to understand what is happening, and the endgame where so few pieces remain that once again one may hope to have some idea of who is winning. The middlegame is thus characterized by a jumbled position with vast numbers of pieces cluttering the board. Trying to understand this part of the game is a hopeless exercise. The only sensible policy is to maintain an expression of pained concentration and total silence instantly hushing anybody who dares ask your opinion of the position. What you are really doing while watching this phase of the game is composing alternative sets of comments to make immediately a result is reached, according to who wins.

Thus, adopting the normal procedure that all moves of the lucky winner are to be praised and all moves of the loser condemned, you must prepare two (or three if really conscientious to include the possibility of a draw) sets of comments extolling the virtues and decrying the insufficiencies of each move played by both sides. A typical pair of alternatives is: 'Desperation, but white was lost anyway', and 'A fine combination, rounding off a well-played attack'. One of these annotations may be appended to any sacrifice according simply to whether it works or not.

If you watch leading chess journalists watching tournament games, never be fooled into thinking that they are working out what is happening in the positions. They are just knocking their comments into shape to be ready when the games finish. Easy once you have the knack.

The Endgame

Here you must be careful. Bluffing is easy in the opening, where mock erudition is as good as the real thing, and not so hard, with the benefit of hindsight, in the middlegame. But the endgame can be a precise science where one might be expected not only to know what is happening but to be able to demonstrate and justify one's conclusions. The only policy here is to avoid giving any precise opinion on the position under discussion. Refer instead to similar positions, where one's knowledge will not be undermined by anything that might happen in the game. The typical conversation might run something like this.

'That's a difficult rook ending. Is it a win?'

'Well, if the white f-pawn were on the g-file, there would be no doubt, but of course, on the f-file it can be different.'

'What's the difference?'

'There's more room to the right of the f-file than the g-file.'

'Does he win if it's a g-pawn?'

'Well, it's certainly a win if the pawn is far enough advanced.'

'Oh, they've just agreed a draw.'

'Yes, I thought that extra file would make all the difference.'

That really is all there is to know about endgame theory. The positions you want to know about are never in the books anyway, so why bother studying them when you can be just as impressive without the effort.

12. Somewhat Compromised

I do not approve of guys using false pretences on dolls, except, of course, when nothing else will do.
Damon Runyon

One night I am passing the corner of Red Square in the city of Moscow, Russia, thinking of taking a walk around to big Lenny's mausoleum, when along comes a very tasty-looking young doll. In fact she is a doll with red hair, and personally I maintain there is no sight more soothing than a doll with red hair. Now I wish to say that I see some dolls in my time but this one has a way of moving like I do not know what. Personally I am very impressed and consider she is 100 per cent in every respect, and as she passes she grins at me very pleasant.

To tell the truth I admit for a second I think she is maybe somewhat ginned up, then all of a sudden she says to me like this:

'Pardon me,' the doll says, only she says it in Russian and I translate for the benefit of the reader, 'do you fancy a tumble across the chessboard?'

Now when I hear this I wish to say I am more than somewhat surprised as I never see a doll carry on like this in Moscow, Russia, without a formal invitation, but she looks the sort of Natasha who plays a good game of chess so I smile and say yes. We set off together down Borovitsky Hill past St Basil's with the doll leading the way.

Well, after a couple of minutes walking she says we are there and we climb two flights of stairs, and then she opens a door and tells me to come in. I am very happy, personally, that we

finally get somewhere because I do not like this walking in the snow. Then I see something in the doll's eyes which tells me she is still feeling like playing chess and I am commencing to be glad I am present.

She does not say much, not being the sort of doll who goes a packet on conversation, but takes me by the arm and leads me into her bedroom, at least I suppose it is her bedroom because it has a big bed in the middle of the floor and smells like a perfume shop. I look around a bit but not so you think I am intruding my nose where it does not belong and I see some very nice bits of clothes and jewellery and suchlike lying about such as must have cost a few bananas. I figure this doll must be something special since she is by no means married and you need plenty of coconuts to keep a joint of this class a going concern.

Well she puts the chessboard on the bed and as I am at all times a gentleman I naturally insist that the doll has white. She plays pawn to king four which I regard as a bad sign. I do not care for pawn to king four openings under any circumstances and she begins to have a strange expression on her kisser. I decide I have to outplay her on the level and I play my king pawn likewise. Then she comes out with her knight. In such a game as this I do not reckon on a doll who is fully booked up and I am commencing to grow nervous. She wants to hospitalize my pawn but I figure that if I cannot give a pawn to the prettiest thing that ever steps in shoe leather then I am not worth the title of master which the Federation gives me. Anyway it is never my policy to discourage any doll who wishes to strike up an acquaintance with me, which is what I reckon this doll is trying to do, so I do not defend my pawn and thereby incidentally avoid meeting the Spanish Lopez with which I do not have much truck.

So the doll takes my pawn and laughs and she has a way of laughing which can make Red Tolya leave the party. Then she says she is a bit warm at the present time and she feels for her buttons behind her back, finds same, undoes them and peels off a woollen garment and tosses it aside. She is about 40 per cent in and 60 per cent out of a silk blouse or if it is not silk it certainly cost a few potatoes. I agree it is warm and I remove my jacket and tie.

Well, a few moves later I am not concentrating too well and I overlook a knight. She hangs her cargo of lure over the board and takes it. Harry the horse is dropped into the box, as dead as a frozen shrimp. I wish to say I am not yet worrying about the game but I think I must take the business with a touch more seriousness. The doll spots a change in the expression on my pan and suggests I take off my shoes if I am not comfortable. I do not wish to cause a slight bit of offence, so I am a gentleman and I remove my socks also. She for her part pops another button on her blouse. Two moves later I drop a bishop. At the present time my position disturbs me no little and I judge she is not doing bad for a doll.

Well I am just developing this good-looking counter-attack when I look across the board to see the doll stepping out of her skirt. She does not say a word but plants her curves back on the bed wearing only undergarments such as ladies wear.

Then one of my rooks is hurt pretty bad and croaks a move later. I am about to suggest in a polite manner that I play better if the doll covers her slim young form which is setting fire to my arterial system, when the curtains shoot open. Two guys are standing there watching me and one of them has a camera pointed in my direction. The doll leans over to be sure her best profile gets in the picture and he snaps us together with the board and pieces. They are big guys and look about as homely as a pair of puff adders. I am a good judge of guys' characters and I figure they are not in the holiday snap business. The one who talks introduces himself as a friend of Red Tolya's and suggests that maybe I like to tell him Big Tony's new move in the Dragon.

Well I try to say that Big Tony does not tell me what he analyses, but he suggests that it is better for me if I remember. Naturally a guy such as this is difficult to argue with at the present time because he says he sends the photograph to the Federation. It is far from the best thing in the world for me if the Federation see the picture. I am a rook, knight, bishop and pawn down against a young doll such as ought not to play too

good but here she is carving me up like a turkey. They do not send me to any more international tournaments if they see the pig's ear I make against this doll when I am not even scotched up.

I have to think quick because I do not know Big Tony's move and even if I do I am still at all times a gentleman and cannot tell. Well, the chances are these guys cannot tell a rook's pawn from a frog spawn, being as they seem to carry their weight elsewhere than in their brains, so I tell them that Big Tony's move is king rook to bishop one. They write it down and tell me that it better be right or the Federation will get the picture. I am glad they do not know that king rook to bishop one is older than the fight between Bad Boris and Tiger Tigran back in '69. So I put my shoes on pronto and catch the first plane anywhere.

Back home I personally am not worried. I figure that light bulb is not more than 75 watt. And with a Russian camera at a hundredth of a second on f5.6, who is able to see what happens in the position?

13. Nothing to Lose but Your Pawns

'Totalitarianism in Britain could never work. How could it when nothing else does?' (Alan Coren). Discuss.
Cambridge University Entrance Examination Question

It was a bright cold day in Hastings and the chess clocks ticked with their tentative limping tin voices. Five minutes earlier the Minister of State for Indoor Sports other than Backgammon had concluded his opening speech to polite applause from the gathering of elderly spectators. They had learned that the minister, though not a chessplayer himself, liked the occasional game of darts, so was fully in tune with the competitive demands of the game. A fully adequate speech by normal standards, but some regretted that they had been unable to secure the services of the Minister for Backgammon herself. Unfortunately she had a prior booking to appear in a charity strip show at Eastbourne.

The onlookers settled as best they could into the uncomfortable wooden chairs. Some lurched into conversations with old acquaintances whom they had not seen since the year before, but these were hushed into silence as soon as they began by the stentorian command of the tournament director. None questioned the need for silence, though one or two of the younger members of the audience did allow the thought to cross their minds, in view of the fact that there were no longer any players to disturb. There had been no players now at Hastings since the general strike called by the chessplaying unions five years earlier. But traditions had to be upheld. The opening and closing ceremonies continued and between them the spectators

still attended as absorbed as ever in the historic atmosphere of the event.

Opinions differed as to the reasons which were responsible for bringing about the strike. Some blamed militants within the chessplaying unions. Others traced the malaise back to the reorganization of the British Chess Federation in the late 1970s when they had replaced their cumbersome system of committees by a management board. This step was later to be described as 'provocative' in the inaugural statement which marked the formation of the chessplayers' unions.

Indeed, with the hindsight we now have given to us by historical perspective, it becomes plain that the creation of Management was the trigger which gave impetus to the unionization of chessplayers. Though there had been rumblings for many years among members of the chess labour movement there was no concerted activity until that time. Then apparently spontaneous mass meetings suddenly took place throughout the country. Those who earned their livings or reputations at the game loudly declared solidarity with one another against the dictatorship and exploitation of Management. Not that the British Chess Federation had actually taken any unpopular decisions, or indeed any decisions at all, but solidarity was clearly the right thing to declare at the time.

Men experienced in union matters were quick to come forward with advice. So, using the models of other well-organized working groups, the chessplayers, or chesspiece operatives as they were known, formed themselves into five distinct unions to represent the various skilled and unskilled sectors of the trade.

Initial omens were quite encouraging for the prospects of the newly unionized players. There was a small dispute early on, when the Polity for Precision Pawn Pushing Personnel were unable to reach agreement on differentials with the more prestigious Movers Union (Major Pieces). The introduction of legislation forbidding discrimination in pay between piecework and pawn pay led to industrial action by MUMPs members. We can all remember the famous Hastings that year when only pawns were moved. The hasty government action on that occasion aroused such hostility that the pawn movers of PPPPP quickly came out in sympathy. The joint strike led to the formation of strong bonds between the unions. In a historic announcement, they finally agreed to amalgamate in a spirit of consensus in order to minimize relative deprivation and continue together the struggle to optimize parameters of remuneration.

With the abolition of demarcation lines, all restrictive practices were terminated and members of both unions were allowed to move any pieces they wished. The new rationalized structure incorporated all piece or pawn movers. It called itself the Federated Union of Chess Move Executants. Naturally the members of FUCME were very pleased to have ended their inter-role conflict, but their newly found solidarity and strength led to an increased militancy and did little to smooth the strained relationships with the other chess unions.

The semi-skilled members of FUCME, of course, had only to move the pieces. The skilled labour of deciding where they should be moved was the domain of the more highly paid Confederation of Chess Analysts, Thinkers and Theorists, the white-collar (or more often grey tee-shirt) members of the Association of Chess Horological Operatives, known commonly as MACHOmen, or more pejoratively as the clock-bashers. Thus the CCATT man would decide what move was to be played and duly inform the FUCME representative of his decision. On completion of the task, the FUCME representative alerts his colleague from MACHO, who, with due ceremony, bashes the clock. Finally the move is transcribed onto the score-sheet by the man from SCRIPT, the Society of Chess Record Inscribers, Printers and Tabulators.

Despite some initial hostility from Management, these working practices functioned well and created a great deal of employment. The Government's job-creation programme declared itself very pleased with the new system. Chessboards did, however, tend to become a little crowded, but this seemed a small price to pay for peace. Even when the semi-skilled and unskilled unions came to re-negotiate manning levels, Management conceded their demands with good grace. After all, it

was unreasonable in the present climate, to expect a single man to operate the pieces, or press the clock, or even write the moves for both sides in a game. Having separate union men for each player was a sensible rationalization concomitant with production capacity, as a joint union spokesman put it. The agreement was finalized at a manning level of eight workers to each board.

The great dispute began one year during the British Championship. The Management Disciplinary Committee had been convened to hear a protest following one of the first round games. The loser had complained that no CCATT member was present on the other side. Since the new manning levels had only recently been agreed, and transitional seating regulations were still in force at the board, he had not realized, what with so many people coming and going, that the opposition had only consisted of three union men. Investigations after the game had confirmed that the FUCME operative had been making moves in the absence of instructions from any member of CCATT.

The Disciplinary Committee summoned the accused side, who admitted that there had indeed been no analyst, thinker or theorist prescribing the actions of their FUCME man. Accordingly, the Disciplinary Committee considered that they had no alternative but to expel the offenders from the tournament. After consulting their lawyers, however, and with the full support of the FUCME union, their man sued the Management for wrongful dismissal.

The case made legal history and dragged on for months. The reason for dismissal seemed simple enough: that the FUCME representative had contravened his terms of employment by indulging in a work practice specifically excluded from his contractual obligations – viz: thinking. His defence, however, was equally uncomplicated: that he had played the moves without thinking. Expert witnesses were called by both sides to establish whether one could win a chess game without recourse to processes of thought, theory or analysis. Statisticians proved that it was unlikely; psychologists maintained that it was unthinkable, but the crucial evidence was on the side of the dismissed man. When the judges came to examine

POLICE INTERVENED WHEN FLYING PICKETS STARTED MOVING DIAGONALLY INSTEAD OF...

35 MOVE DAY OR

exhibits demonstrating just how horribly chess can be played when the participants do think about the moves, they found themselves unable to exclude the possibility that one might conceivably do better without thinking at all. The dismissed man was reinstated and awarded compensation. Costs were awarded against Management.

The judgement had immediate and far-reaching repercussions. The skilled CCATT union had been dealt a heavy blow. FUCME submitted a claim for large wage rises, claiming an immediate establishment of parity with the CCATT members. The courts had established that their job was more important than thinking; the thinkers, theoreticians and analysts had lost credibility. MACHO and SCRIPT also demanded large rises, to preserve differentials, they said. Management suggested talks, and were accused of complete intransigence, pursuing a repressive and divisive path to social disruption and economic collapse, and a lack of commitment inconsistent with right-minded awareness.

'We will not talk,' said a joint spokesman for the unskilled unions, 'until there is money on the chess table. We demand across the board increases.'

The Management Board of the Federation reacted cautiously, suggesting that any increases could only be linked to local productivity schemes. More money could only be forthcoming if it meant more moves. Union officials were furious. 'We are furious,' they exclaimed. 'Management seems hellbent on a collision course.' In a statement, they issued new demands for a 35-move day, with overtime for adjournment sessions.

CCATT men were also angered by talk of increased productivity. More moves by FUCME members would necessarily demand more thinking by their own members. Despite the earlier court ruling it was still generally accepted as a traditional trade practice that pieces could not be moved without the consent of a CCATT member. All that was under dispute was the value in financial terms of the thought, analysis or theory which he could provide. The threat to the work quota of CCATT members immediately caused them to down pieces and join the strike call for a 35-move day.

Long periods of negotiation followed, but all have been totally fruitless. Relationships between management and unions became still more strained when an independent time-and-motion study was published claiming that streamlining the industrial practices could result in greater move productivity for less thought. The unions did their own calculations and concluded that British thought was the most productive in the world, in real terms.

So the strike went on. Pickets from all the unions appeared at the doors of all major chess events in the country, attempting to prevent the delivery of chess sets, boards and clocks and to dissuade non-union labour from operating chessmen. 'We shall bring the Federation to its knees,' said a spokesman. 'Chess life is already at a complete standstill. We are at this moment in time in a negative chess situation.'

And so it has been for the past three years. Since the ban on imports of foreign players, there has been no chess played in the land. Latest moves indicate a slim hope that all sides will agree to send the dispute for adjudication. There is even a chance that the forthcoming Royal Commission report may contain the seeds for a settlement.

Until then, however, we rely on the ELO computer to bring us round-by-round tournament results. By this means titles continue to be awarded, prizes won and reputations enhanced. Some of the spectators even prefer the new system. After all, as long as the sporting interest is maintained and the glorious traditions still flourish, why bother with the troublesome necessity of taxing one's brains to try to comprehend the moves. The players were, at the best of times, just an expensive luxury; were they ever really necessary? Long live tradition!

Index